Unforgivable

Unforgivable

COLLETTE ELLIOTT

PENGUIN BOOKS

PENGUIN BOOKS

Published by the Penguin Group
Penguin Books Ltd, 80 Strand, London WC2R ORL, England
Penguin Group (USA) Inc., 375 Hudson Street, New York, New York 10014, USA
Penguin Group (Canada), 90 Eglinton Avenue East, Suite 700, Toronto, Ontario, Canada M4P 2Y3
(a division of Pearson Penguin Canada Inc.)
Penguin Ireland, 25 St Stephen's Green, Dublin 2, Ireland (a division of Penguin Books Ltd)
Penguin Group (Australia), 707 Collins Street, Melbourne, Victoria 3008, Australia
(a division of Pearson Australia Group Pty Ltd)
Penguin Books India Pvt Ltd, 11 Community Centre, Panchsheel Park, New Delhi – 110 017, India
Penguin Group (NZ), 67 Apollo Drive, Rosedale, Auckland 0632, New Zealand
(a division of Pearson New Zealand Ltd)
Penguin Books (South Africa) (Pty) Ltd, Block D, Rosebank Office Park,
181 Jan Smuts Avenue, Parktown North, Gauteng 2193, South Africa

Penguin Books Ltd, Registered Offices: 80 Strand, London WC2R ORL, England

www.penguin.com

First published 2014
005

Set in 12.5/14.75pt Garamond MT Std
Typeset by Jouve (UK), Milton Keynes
Printed in Great Britain by Clays Ltd, St Ives plc

ISBN: 978-1-405-91823-7

www.greenpenguin.co.uk

MIX
Paper from
responsible sources
FSC® C018179

Penguin Books is committed to a sustainable
future for our business, our readers and our planet.
This book is made from Forest Stewardship
Council™ certified paper.

To Rachel
I will never forget what you whispered in my ear

Prologue

Mother flashed her green eyes at me.

'When we get in here, just you do as you're told, OK?'

I nodded, but she had already turned to face the door. It opened and a chubby-faced man was standing there.

'Come in, come in,' he said, his eyes darting up and down the street.

We went inside. It looked quite a nice house. There weren't the same dirty stains on the carpet or the same stench of smoke as in our place.

Mother had told me the man was called Larry. He was one of her friends. Mother had lots of men friends, even after we had gone to live with Dave. This one lived with his mother. I know this because she left the house not long after we walked into the front room and Larry called: 'Right, Mum. Leave us in peace.'

We had only been inside for a few short moments but already Mother had raised her voice to Larry's mum, a big lady who didn't take kindly to being spoken to like that in her own home. That's what she said.

Mother was always doing that – upsetting people, shouting at them. It never took her long to lose her temper.

After she'd gone, Mother and Larry sat on the sofa. I was on an armchair in the bay window. I wondered if I would be offered a biscuit. Some of Mother's friends gave me chocolate biscuits like Wagon Wheels while they sat and chatted. It didn't look like I was going to be offered one today, though.

Without much of a warning Mother and Larry started kissing each other. Their loud, slurpy kisses drowned out the noise of the ticking clock on the mantelpiece. I wanted to turn away but found I couldn't avert my eyes. Larry's breathing started getting heavier and his kissing became more intense. His hands were all over Mother's body, from her hair, around her neck, down her chest and up her legs. As he moved them more frantically, it looked like he had more than two. They were everywhere.

Then they started taking off their clothes. At first Larry tried to take Mother's top off her but then she took over and started removing it herself. While she was doing that he took off his shirt, then his shoes and socks, and he started unbuckling his belt.

Mother stood up and pushed down her trousers.

'Just you look out the window, will you?' she said to me.

I swung round and stared outside. There wasn't much going on in the street. Some parked cars, a couple of mums pushing buggies, two other people a bit further up, chatting. I wondered if they knew what was going on in here. I looked at the other houses and wondered if inside them other people were carrying on like these two were in here.

Behind me I could hear Mother and Larry breathing even more heavily and now they were groaning too. There was a bit of fumbling and cursing and then the groaning became more rhythmic. I now know, of course, what was happening but back then I didn't have a clue. It didn't sound pleasant, whatever it was.

I tried staring out of the window but couldn't focus on anything except the noises behind me. I had a slight urge to turn round but I knew what would happen if Mother caught me. Plus, something told me I wouldn't like what I saw.

It seemed like it went on for hours but it was probably only a few minutes. Larry's groaning got faster. I thought he might be hurting himself and was about to turn round to see what the fuss was about, but then it stopped.

Mother's breathing returned to normal quickly. She never seemed out of breath for long. It must have been all that walking around the estate she did. Larry's was a bit more laboured. He sounded like he'd been running for a bus.

Only when it was over and their breathing had returned to normal did Mother speak to me.

'Right, you can turn round now,' she said. They were

fastening up their clothes. Larry looked red in the face. He was smoothing his hair back over.

Now things were back to normal I wondered if I might get that biscuit. We weren't hanging around, however. No sooner had Mother got dressed again than she said: 'Come on, Col. We're leaving now.'

We went to the door.

'See ya,' Mother said.

We walked home, Mother powering ahead, my little legs struggling to keep up. We got to our flat. As we went through the main door, Mother turned, those eyes flashing again.

'Don't you breathe a word of this to Dave, you hear?' she said. 'You tell him about where we've been and I'll kill ya.'

I

As a parent it's a natural instinct to love, protect and nurture our children. When they fall we pick them up and kiss the pain away; when they have bad dreams we hold them tight until they feel safe. We do everything we can to encourage our children to explore life and make decisions. If they falter we help put the pieces back together. In the animal kingdom the rules are just the same: mothers protect their young with any means necessary.

Most mothers say they learned how to deal with the challenging schedules of being a parent through a combination of instinct and the wisdom of the generations before them. I have many friends who have turned to their own mothers for this support and guidance. I wish I could say the same.

I do not recall my mother ever holding my hand, even as a little girl. She never cuddled me when I was sick, never told me she loved me, never told me I was precious.

Instead my mother demonstrated her passion in other ways – by lashing out. Usually she slapped and kicked, but sometimes she pulled clumps of hair out and, occasionally, she bit me. Sometimes I would fight back but it always felt wrong. Despite her cruelty she drummed into me that a child had to respect its parents.

Plus, Mother was always fond of saying: 'I brought you into this world and I can take you out with one click of my fingers.'

Christmases and birthdays, happy family holidays, a special day out or just cuddles on the sofa before bedtime – I don't have any of these memories. Not big ones, certainly. For me, happiness came in a fleeting, sometimes stolen moment, rather than being always there, even in the background.

It's not that I can't remember that far back. Sometimes my memory works too well. However, trying to recall some of my earliest moments can be like trying to fit the pieces together in a jigsaw puzzle.

I know I was born at Marston Green Hospital, in Birmingham, on a Thursday night, 7 September 1977, a hospital that has since been pulled down. I don't know how much I weighed but I do know my mother's waters broke while she was on a bus going over Cuckoo Bridge in the city. Luckily, she was with her sister, who managed to get her to the hospital. I don't have any other details about the birth – such things a mother shares with her first-born. I just arrived.

Mother brought me home to Nechells, an inner-city area characterized by high-rise tower blocks. It was where many of her family lived, so she had all the help she needed.

Mother's name was Maureen. She was a very slim blonde, not unattractive, but with a mouth that could spit venom. She possessed the green eyes of a monster, from which a glare or flash could send many people running for cover. She wouldn't think twice about shouting, swearing or even fighting in public. When she was in a mood everyone knew about it. Even her own family received the lash of her tongue and tantrums. She often fought with her siblings and parents and never showed any remorse.

My grandparents used to tell me that they would only see Mother when she wanted something – usually money – and they felt the less they saw of her the better. Mother got involved in so many fights they would have implications for her sisters: Mother's enemies would target her siblings as a way of getting back at her – even jumping them as a way of hammering the message home – but she didn't care. Rather than apologize for the grief she had caused, she would often laugh.

There were times when I was growing up when I thought she was pushing everyone away from her, but the reality was that she had burned her bridges with her family long before I was even born.

When she was twenty-four, she began a relationship with a petty criminal called Philip who she had known since she was a teenager. Theirs was a very volatile relationship. Mother would often end up with black eyes, sprained wrists or fat lips. Phil was in and out of prison all the time for robbing people's homes and cars. I'm not offering excuses for his actions, but he did what he did to survive, to put food on the table.

On one occasion when he was locked up Mother started hanging around with different crowds of people. Phil would send round his family and friends to check she was behaving herself. What he didn't know was that Mother was a prostitute and these people were her clients.

Despite Phil's efforts to keep her in check, she continued to meet men. She got careless and as a result fell pregnant with me. From what I can gather she was petrified of how Phil would react. However, when she told him she was expecting he was delighted. He knew the baby wasn't his but he didn't care. I was named Collette Marie after Phil's sister Marie, who also became my godmother. When I was born they both doted on me, I was told. In the early days, at least.

They shared a flat on the first floor of a tower block in Nechells and socialized with the same circle of friends with which they had grown up. Mother used to call Phil and his friends 'teddy boys' – they had the quiff and leather jacket and coloured shoes, whether black, blue or red, to match their outfit.

My grandparents hoped my arrival might bring Mother and Phil closer together and for a while it seemed it had. Their hopes were soon dashed, however. Before long, they began torturing each other. As much as he loved me, Phil could never forgive my mother for cheating, and the beatings she endured, I was told, were quite vicious.

And Phil's rage didn't stop with Mother. He would often threaten my granddad when he dared to defend his daughter. The sight of her injuries upset my nan – this was her baby and she felt she couldn't do anything to stop him. Phil never once took his anger out on me, though. To him, I was always his baby. When he was around, he protected me. When he wasn't, I was at the mercy of my mother.

And as was to prove the case again and again over the years, that wasn't a safe place for any child but, least of all, for me.

2

By rights, I shouldn't be here. I should be another stat-istic. A case you read about in the papers, like Baby P or Daniel Pelka – children who died as a result of horrible brutality and neglect.

I almost didn't see my fourth birthday.

My memory doesn't go back that far. I was a little child, after all, but over the years, from testimony from relatives and, finally, after reading my own social-work files, I discovered the horrible truth about an incident that happened when I was just three years old.

Mother was supposed to be looking after me. We were alone together in her flat, which at the time was on the first floor of a block. She had been out the night before until 3 a.m., leaving me in the care of a strange man. In the morning he had disappeared and Mother was lying on the bed, out for the count. Somehow, as she lay in a comatose state, I climbed on to the window ledge in the bedroom, opened the window and fell out.

A neighbour found me lying on the ground outside. Unconscious.

Mother only knew something had happened when someone knocked on the door with my limp body in his arms. I had fractured my skull and broken my leg, but I was alive – and incredibly lucky to have survived the fall.

The police were called. Mother maintained that she had been in the kitchen and knew nothing about what had happened.

'I only took my eye off her for a second,' she said. 'You know what kids are like.'

Other family members offered their own conclusions. When I was growing up they told me about the incident and said Mother would often go out, leaving me – a three-year-old kid – to fend for myself.

Mother hardly spoke about it. She just brushed it off if it was mentioned. I was alive, wasn't I? What did I have to complain about?

As I grew up I knew it was a serious incident but I began to buy Mother's line that it was 'one of those things', that it could have happened to anyone, that it was a 'one-off'.

It wasn't. Not long afterwards, a neighbour saw me standing on the window ledge again. One step and I could have plummeted to the ground. That time, I might not have been so lucky.

It took me a very long time – and nearly a lifetime of abuse, neglect, anguish and suffering that pushed me to the point of taking my own life, not once, but several times – to find out the truth about my early childhood.

There have been times when I wished I hadn't been

so 'incredibly lucky', when I wished that I had died that day. I began to believe what Mother never tired of telling me: 'You should never have been born.'

Vague, fractured memories haunted me like bad dreams. I recall being on my own in a dark flat calling for Mummy, but no one answered. I remember looking around and seeing only the faces of strange men. Mother was nowhere to be seen. When she was there, which sometimes wasn't often, she was angry and violent, hitting me. Often I had no idea what I had done wrong. I remember being passed around, from pillar to post. Maybe that was why I was never shy around strangers and was always looking for a friendly face. That was something I just didn't get at home.

But these were just memories. When I finally found out the real story of my life, it was more shocking than anything I'd been told as a youngster. And, believe me, some of that was bad enough.

My granddad once told me that he was so sickened by Mother's behaviour towards me that he told her if I had died that day when I had fallen out of the window she would have had to leave Birmingham for good. My grandparents said that, as a result of that incident, I stayed with them a lot.

You might think such an episode would be a wake-up call for Mother, but she carried on being as reckless as before. It was as if she just didn't care, about me, about anything. Phil was still in and out of prison, so my grandparents bought all my outfits and made sure I was clean, fed and healthy. That's what they told me at the time, anyway.

Mother's prostitution landed her in court several times, prompting social services to become concerned that she was unfit to care for me. I was told they took me into care when I was eighteen months old and again when I was two. Mother had such disrespect for authority that, apparently, my grandparents were made my legal guardians. Exactly how this came about and what happened when I was taken into care and how I got out was a mystery to me for a long time.

So, for much of my life, I chose instead to focus on those fleeting moments and sensations of happiness. I had to have something to cling on to.

Despite being in and out of her care, some of my earliest memories are of being with Mother and being dragged around the shops. I recall her stopping at every *Evening Mail* stall to talk to the vendor and chatting to a man at a stall that sold potatoes in the winter and ice creams in the summer. The potatoes were tiny and cooked in a black, old-style oven. The man would use a scoop and put them in a white paper cone. I can remember covering them in loads of salt and scraping my finger along the bottom of the cone before licking off the white grains. My tongue would burn but the taste was worth the pain. In summer, he kept his ice cream in blocks in a freezer. He would cut it to fit a cone and sometimes I'd have more than one flavour. Mother liked her ice cream between two wafers.

Another thing I remember vividly was the number of punk rockers we'd see, with their spiky hair of many colours. I was absolutely petrified of them and Mother said I screamed whenever I saw one walking down the street. I used to hide in the grit bins until they had passed. Mother said one day I screamed so much she threatened to leave me in a phone box. I couldn't stop so she carried out her threat. The phone boxes back then were big and red with a door so heavy you had to use both hands to prise it open. Mother put me in a phone box and walked off. She said she could see me the whole time but left me in there to teach me a lesson. I don't know how long I was in there.

These are some of the only genuine memories I have of my mother from this time, because she was hardly ever there. I have cloudy recollections of sitting on my own, on cold, hard stone stair landings while Mother was inside with a man friend.

Other times she disappeared, leaving me amid a sea of strange faces – all of them men's. I had no idea who these people were or what their intentions were.

Some of my happiest moments from this period, unsurprisingly, come from the times I wasn't with my mother, like the times I spent at my nan's. My uncle Darren and aunt Wendy still lived at home and the house was always full of their friends. Darren used to swing me round by my arms and Nan would shout at him, saying, 'You'll pull her arms out of her sockets,' but I loved it. I'd jump up and down, begging him to do it again, and when Nan's back was turned he would. I would fall to the ground dizzy, laughing so hard my belly would hurt. I looked up to my uncle. He took me to the park to play football with his mates. He hid from me once and I thought he'd left me so I screamed. He thought it was hilarious but when I told Nan she whacked him round the ear so hard it turned purple.

Wendy was more grown up – she was fifteen years older than me, after all. We'd sit in my nan's lounge blasting the stereo out and listening to music. We had a shared love of tomatoes and would cover them in salt and sit on the sofa munching them from a bag from the greengrocer's. We all loved Wendy. My cousins and I would argue about who was going to stay the weekend with her. I would often get to stay, because Mother would be out doing her own thing.

Inevitably, her relationship with Phil came to an end. Once that happened, Granddad didn't trust Mother to look after me. At least when Phil was on the scene, he knew I would come to no harm, but with him gone I'd be at the mercy of Mother – and he knew all too well what that would mean. As for Phil, he was devastated when Mother ended it. His flat was like a shrine to me – every inch of the wall covered in pictures – and once it was over he hit the bottle. Eventually, he turned to drugs in a big way.

Despite the chaos of my early years, I did attend nursery. It was a five-minute walk from Nan's and I loved it. I remember having jam sandwiches for lunch and nearly always sitting on the slide. On the afternoons I attended Mother would collect me and take me to meet Nan from work. There was a shop opposite the nursery that sold everything from fruit and vegetables to knitting wool. It was a tiny shop and the owner was lovely. She had big wavy red hair and freckles that covered her face. She was always smiling and, though sometimes I wouldn't return her smiles, she still beamed, like sunshine. Every day she would stop us as we passed to give me a freshly cleaned carrot. Not only did I love tomatoes, I loved carrots too. Mother said I would moan until she went in the shop to get me one and the lady got so used to us going in there every day that she would have the carrot prepared for me for when I came out of nursery.

These were the happy moments I clung on to – the episodes that made me realize there *was* fun in the world. Perhaps I was too young then to remember the bad times. Perhaps I blotted them out.

All I know is that I enjoyed some of those early days with my grandparents, aunt, uncle and cousins.

I only wish it had lasted. It was from the age of four that the nightmares began.

3

It almost seems like a dream, like I am watching grainy old video footage of another family – a family where love and laughter were taken for granted. They are my memories, however, of a happy family. It just wasn't my family.

When I was four years old social services placed me into foster care. Because I was so young at the time, my memories are hazy, but it was with a family with other children. I don't remember their names and can't really picture their faces. But I do remember – so vividly – the love they had for each other and, it seemed, for me.

I think I was one of three children placed there. I remember the house quite well. There was a dining room and the heart of the home was a large table where everyone would sit together and laugh during mealtimes. Such memories stand out so clearly because they were so rare in my life. I can also picture myself sitting on the floor playing with a spinning top. For hours, it seemed, I would sit watching the pictures on it twirl around.

The main lounge was reserved for the evenings when, after we had had tea, had a bath and put our pyjamas on, we would snuggle together on the floor, lying on our tummies with our legs swinging in the air and our hands under our chins, and watch a film. The first movie I saw in full was *ET*, about the alien stranded on Earth, trying to find his way back home. I'd never seen a movie before and was amazed at the effects and the drama. It was so real. I was a little bit scared, but I jumped on to my foster mother's lap and buried my face into her cardigan. As she stroked my hair and hugged me tightly to her, I felt safe.

The garden was huge. Until then the only garden I'd been able to play in was the one at my nan's, but that was nothing like this. One day one of the other foster kids made a car out of wood and cardboard boxes. I watched him pretend to drive it and imagined the two of us driving down fast lanes. We'd pretend he was taking me to the shops, and I'd get out, walk up the garden and come back before I got into the car again for the drive home. It was brilliant. It kept us amused for hours.

Every Sunday our foster parents would take us to church. We'd all pile into the 'big car' and set off with a Murray Mint to suck on for the journey. Even today, when I eat one of those sweets I smile. The taste brings back such happy memories. Sometimes these memories were all I had to sustain me through my darkest hours.

I still saw my mother, once or twice a week. I don't really remember much about her in those days, though. She was hardly ever there.

I saw more of my social worker, Penny, who *was*, it seemed, always there to pick me up. She'd take me to a children's centre on Castle Vale, not far from Erdington, to the north-east of central Birmingham. Penny had a kind face, warm eyes and always smelled nice. She smiled at me, crouched down to my level and talked to me the way I saw other kids' mums talk to their children. She always stayed with us during our visits. She was just lovely – someone I wanted to be my real mum.

If it was warm we'd stay outside and play on the see-saw. Sometimes my uncle Darren would come, and he would chase me around the grass until I'd fall over with laughter. Sometimes when I had to leave I'd cry. I didn't want to leave. This was how I wanted it to be always. It rarely was, however. I was crying for a dream I had about what life should be like. The reality, though, was that sometimes we'd go to a meeting place and Mother wouldn't show up.

Other times I was so happy in my foster care I didn't want to see Mother at all. I started wetting the bed at night if I knew I was going to see her the next day. I'd put on a smile and pretend I was enjoying myself but really I wanted to be back at my foster parents'. Once I returned there I was happy and never wanted to leave again.

On one occasion I remember being at a meeting with Mother and Penny. I was playing on the floor while they talked among themselves. I fell over and bumped my head and burst into tears. Even though I was crying, I remember hesitating: who should I go to?

Mother looked at me like I was an irritating, yappy little dog. In stark comparison, Penny's features softened in natural concern. There was really no dilemma. It was obvious. I got up and ran to Penny, feeling instantly soothed by the social worker's warm embrace.

One sunny morning, I went downstairs for my breakfast, but after I was dressed I was called into the dining room. My foster parents were sitting at the large dining table with Penny. Their kind faces were smiling at me and, as I sat down, they passed me a cup of juice and some biscuits. The adults chatted for what seemed like for ever but then, suddenly, they were involving me in the conversation.

'Your mummy is getting married,' my foster mother said. 'You can go to her wedding if you like.'

What? Who was my mother marrying? I didn't have a dad – at least not since Phil had left the scene – so how would that work? Did this mean I was going to have a new daddy? Questions came gushing out of my mouth in torrents. I was four years old. I didn't have a clue what was going on, or when it was going to happen.

They took me into the back garden, held my hand and led me up to the back fence and to the gate we were never allowed to go through. This time, however, the gate was being opened. Beyond was where all the flowers were. I was amazed at how many there were. I had never seen anything like it. There were daisies so tall they could have been sunflowers, they were so big and colourful. My foster father cut some for me, wrapped the stems in foil and said I could take them for my mother's wedding.

It was a deeply confusing time. My mother represented something I longed for, but being with my foster family made me happy in a way I'd never experienced before. Here was a family that truly wanted me. They were the kindest people I had ever met and they made me feel that I was part of a family. I felt 'normal'.

I wore a red velvet dress for the wedding ceremony, but I cried my eyes out in the car to the registry office.

Mother was marrying a man named Steve. The first time I met him was at their wedding. He was thin and wiry with a moustache. He seemed nice enough that day. Mother looked lovely and seemed happy with him. She didn't really pay much attention to me but I remember her telling me one thing. I was going to live with them in his flat.

I was torn. I didn't want to leave the warmth and safety of my foster family – but if marrying Steve meant Mum was happier, then would that mean life with her would be better? All I could do was hope.

I didn't get the chance to say goodbye to my foster family. Instead, I cherish the memory of walking with them among the daisies as our farewell.

Being with Mother and Steve was good to begin with. They took me to Steve's flat and showed me my room, which he'd decorated with white walls with a pink border and a rose-pink carpet. My quilt cover had a huge picture of a dolly on it and next to my bed was a white table with a pretty pink lamp. At bedtime Steve read me a story about Rupert the Bear and for a few days it became a nightly occurrence. Life was good, I thought. I was starting to enjoy being with Mum again. She didn't shower me with the same hugs and kisses as my foster mum, but she was there and, at the time, that was all that mattered.

After I'd been home a month, Mum started to take me with her to a café where her friend and neighbour Mary worked. We began to spend a lot of time there. Mary lived in the flat above us and if we weren't in the café we'd be in Mary's flat. It was quite strange. She didn't have furniture, she had beanbags instead, lots of them, and candles and funny-smelling sticks I now know were incense. She was a fairly large lady with a stud in her nose, wild hair and a laugh that made her whole frame shake. She was always so nice to me. At the café I'd help Mary serve customers by taking their money and handing them their change. I wiped down the tables and swept the floor and for being so helpful I'd get a can of Coke and a Wagon Wheel chocolate biscuit.

Mother, on the other hand, didn't lift a finger. She was constantly in and out, going off with strange men but coming back on her own. One man in particular I used to see every day. He drove a black cab, and whenever Mother went off with him she'd come back with a bruise or a bloody nose or mouth. I felt myself hating this man. One time when Mum came back looking roughed up I shouted to him: 'Leave my mummy alone!'

He shouted something back at me with a nasty snarl on his mouth. I begged my mother not to go with him, but she never listened to me.

'You're just a child,' she said. 'Leave it.'

When we got home that day Steve sent me out to the park by myself. I didn't like going on my own because I didn't know anyone and just sat on the swings watching the other kids play Tag and Stuck in the Mud. After a while Steve shouted out of the block window that it was time to come home. The other kids laughed at me as I made my way meekly through the alleyways to the flat. Steve met me outside the lift, took my arm and threw me through the open door of our flat straight into their bedroom, where Mother was lying completely naked and crying on the bed.

Once I was in the room, Steve locked the door.

'You can stay in here until the morning,' he said, slamming it behind him.

There was a bucket in the corner of the room. That was to be our toilet. Mother's bedroom wasn't warm and comfy like mine. There was a double wardrobe, a double bed, and the bucket, of course, and that was it, so being locked in the room all night wasn't fun. All we could do was sleep.

The next few days were the same. Mum and I would be out for most of the day and when we came home I'd be sent out and when I came back Mum would be crying.

That became our routine. Out during the day and locked in the bedroom at night. I wasn't allowed back in my room. I had to stay in the room with Mother. I never slept in my lovely bedroom, under the pretty duvet cover, again.

One evening my mother flipped and started attacking Steve, punching and kicking and screaming. I ran into my bedroom and could hear them yelling at each other and things being smashed. Steve then came crashing into the room, grabbed me by the arm and shoved me through the open flat door.

Mother was on the ground, beaten to a bloody pulp. She was whimpering like a battered animal. We never said a word to each other; we just got in the lift, still in our nightdresses, left the block and went to a phone box nearby. After Mum made a call, we sat on a wall. Before long a taxi pulled up along with two police cars. I started to feel scared.

At the sight of the police, Mum started shouting and screaming at the officers. Some man was trying to put me into the taxi. He had this huge stick with nails jutting out of it and he was screaming that he'd wrap it around somebody's neck. I started screaming but, for some reason, Mother told me to go with this man. I had never seen him before but I heard her telling the police he was taking me home. Home? Where was that?

It turned out home was Mother's old flat on the

Greenford estate, and the man with the stick was her new boyfriend, Dave. Mother had kept her flat for the six weeks she was married to Steve, and Dave had been living there. I had no idea how that came about, but Dave was there – and very settled, by the looks of it. The flat was tiny. There was a kitchen, a lounge and bedrooms, but my room, compared to my last one, was a box.

In the first few days after we moved in Mother seemed a lot happier and Dave didn't seem as scary as he had that first time I saw him. He had a car and would take us out to country pubs. We used to go to Stratford a lot, because Dave's friend lived there. I wasn't allowed inside the pub so I would stand outside with a glass of Coke. There was a big fir tree next to the pub and I can remember rubbing my fingers on its rough leaves and smelling the pine on my hands. I played with the cones, kicking them up against the wall until they broke.

Dave's mate only lived up the road from the pub and we'd often end up or start there. In his kitchen he kept a motorbike, which I thought was weird.

Dave decorated my room for me with heart-patterned wallpaper, except he hung it upside down. I tried to tell him, but he told me I was wrong and Mother told me to keep my mouth shut.

In the summer, Dave took us on holiday to Great Yarmouth. It was the first time I'd ever been to the beach. We stayed in a little bed and breakfast and it was all a new experience for me. The sounds and smells coming from the fairground seemed to draw me in.

The twinkling lights and the fruit machines throwing out bundles of change, children squealing with delight at the size of the candyfloss – it was a world away from home.

After a few months Dave got me a little puppy. It was a black mongrel and from the moment I set eyes on her furry little face, I adored her. For the first time, I had something that loved me unconditionally. She was always happy to see me and didn't scowl or snap if I did something I wasn't supposed to. I was allowed to name her, so I chose the name of the one person I loved more than anyone else – the woman who seemed to be there for me whenever I needed her: Penny, my social worker.

Mother didn't even seem to notice the connection.

When I turned five Dave and Mum enrolled me into a local primary school. I'd started to go to nursery at three, but I had missed so much I was to be held back for the first year of primary. I loved being part of the class and being able to play with other children. Once I got settled, I seemed to excel and was moved ahead of my year. I made friends with some of the children but never really had a best friend. That seemed to be something other children had, along with so much else.

Being at school helped make me feel normal, but some of Mother's behaviour didn't change. She was still going to the café. Dave didn't know, because he was working, and Mum forced me to keep it a secret.

'He'll leave us if he ever finds out,' she said. I didn't want him to leave, so I kept my mouth shut.

Mother continued to meet different men and started to take me with her. It was on one of these occasions that I went to Larry's house, as I described at the start of the book, and had to look out of the window while they 'entertained' each other.

From that day I'd often be around when Mother met her men friends. More often than not we went to their homes but, sometimes, if Dave was out, she had men come to her. If that happened, Mother would send me outside, to sit on the landing and play on the stairs until it was over.

If she had to go out for a 'quick job' she would leave me with someone, or, if no one was free, leave me on my own. Looking back, it seems absurd to leave a child so young in a house on their own but, at the time, I think I was so used to her not being there that it didn't seem to bother me as much as it might other children.

Other times, Mother took me to the men's houses for the night. She'd tell me to lie on the bed and go to sleep. Then they'd climb into the same bed. I think she thought I was asleep. I certainly pretended to be sleeping, but it was impossible when the bed was jolting up and down and Mother was making groaning noises.

When she wasn't cavorting with me in tow, Mother seemed to be causing trouble wherever she went. Back home, she was constantly arguing with neighbours, smashing windows and fighting in the street. I noticed people were looking at me in the same way they looked at her. I'd sit on the step outside the flat waiting for Mother to kick off again. Everyone knew how unstable she was, and they were too frightened to confront her.

I still saw Penny from time to time. She popped in to see Mother and she would always take time to sit with me and ask how I was. Soon, though, those visits became fewer and fewer. Maybe she thought we were happy now.

One of Mother's friends, June, lived in another block, close to us, but she had a maisonette over two floors, unlike our one-storey flat. June's children were called Donna, Rachel, Sally and Adam. I really liked Donna. She used to take me to the shops and let me sit in her bedroom listening to music. She talked about her boyfriend a lot. Richard was a fireman and Donna told me that they were going to get married and have lots of babies. I never really saw Donna's brother because he was always locked in his bedroom, and Donna used to say he was weird.

In those days, our house was frequently plunged into darkness. This was a time when everyone where we lived had electricity meters that ran on 50p pieces. If you didn't have 50p, you didn't have electricity.

One night I was sitting on the floor in front of the fire, with candles all around. My puppy Penny was with me. In the morning when I got up Penny was gone. The electrics were back on.

'Where's Penny?' I asked Dave.

'She's not here. We had to give her away,' he said. 'She's gone to live on a farm.'

'Oh,' I said. 'I see.' But I didn't see.

'She'll be happier there,' he said.

I was devastated. I didn't even get the chance to say goodbye to her. One minute she was there; the next she was gone. I tried to console myself that she was running around in a huge open space. Years later, Mother told me Dave sold her to pay for the meter.

It was during this period, when I was five, that one evening Mother and Dave said they were going out and had asked June if she would look after me. Mum took me to June's flat with my overnight bag but, when we got there, their home was in darkness. When we went in there were candles everywhere. June and Donna had brought down the mattresses from their beds so they could share the light off the candles and play cards to pass the time. Adam had stayed in his room, and Rachel and Sally were staying with friends.

Later that evening June said she needed to go to the shop. Donna was going with her, because it was dark. I was in my nightdress and Donna called Adam downstairs to watch me for ten minutes. The moment they left Adam looked at me, took one of the candles and blew out the rest and went back upstairs. I was scared on my own in the dark, so I started crying.

'Stop crying and come upstairs,' he shouted. 'It's not so dark here.'

I went upstairs and knocked on his bedroom door. It was slightly ajar and he called me in. He was lying on a mattress on the floor in the corner, the candle next to him.

'Come and sit on the bed,' he said, gesturing for me to join him. I sat down on the edge of the mattress but he pulled me into the middle. I can still recall the feel of his arm around my waist. I knew I had something to be scared about, but I didn't know what. He was holding me like my mother's 'friends' held her. I didn't like the groaning noises she made and I didn't want him to hurt me like the men hurt my mother.

I tried to stand up, but he held on to my waist so tight I felt sick. He suddenly pulled me down and I fell on my back on the mattress. Before I knew what was happening he was lying on top of me. I could smell his sweat as he grinded himself into me.

'Get off me!' I yelled. I shouted and screamed, but I knew no one was coming.

I felt his hand up my nightdress. His long, greasy hair was in my mouth. He started kissing my body and I thought I was going to throw up.

Then there was a bang. Adam jumped up, hurriedly pulled on his top and ran downstairs. It was June and Donna coming back from the shop.

I got up and ran to the top of the stairs. I wanted to tell on Adam, but I froze. What had just happened? What did I tell June? Should I tell my mother?

Donna called me to come down. My legs were shaking

so much I thought I was going to fall over. I could hear my heart pounding in my ears. Slowly, I walked down the stairs and into the lounge. Adam was lighting the candles. I fell on to Donna's bed, and everyone laughed.

'You're a tired little lady,' Donna said. 'It's way past your bedtime.'

I didn't feel tired. I felt sore. I wanted my mum. I wanted to go home.

I didn't sleep a wink that night. I lay on Donna's mattress while she slept with her mum. Every little noise drove me under the covers, convinced Adam was going to come back and hurt me. Where was Mum? Why hadn't she come back for me? I wanted to go home.

In the morning Mum came to collect me, but I never said a word to her, or June, about what happened. Just as Mum kept secrets from Dave in case he left her, I decided I had to keep my mouth shut if I didn't want anything bad to happen to me.

I prayed I wouldn't have to go back there and every night I let out a faint sigh of relief if Mother said she was staying in. She was pregnant by this time, and social services were constantly turning up to make sure she was OK. She slept a lot during the day, so a friend called Carol, who had two sons, Matthew and Michael, used to take me to school. We would race down the road to the school gates. I'd look for them at playtime, but I could never find them. I'd walk home on my own, looking at the houses, daydreaming that one day we would live in a house like theirs.

Mother's new friend, Sue, had moved into the flat below us and she had two children, Stephanie and Lee. Stephanie was my age and at weekends I was allowed to play on the green outside the block with her. Sue was lovely and kind, always cuddling me when she saw me. Their place was always fun. Sometimes I was allowed to stay the night. Stephanie had a TV in her room and so many toys, and Sue would let us play all over the flat. One day we were hairdressers and we soaked the bathroom with the shower and used all the shampoo. On another day we were cooks and pretended to make a curry, putting everything we could think of into the sauce: washing-up liquid, ketchup, sugar, salt, beans – anything we could lay our hands on. Sue never minded if we made a mess. For those brief few hours I felt like a child. It seemed like the only time I was allowed to be one.

At my own house, Mum continued to sleep during the day and when I came home she was in bed, all the curtains drawn. Dave's cup was still on the coffee table from the morning. I pulled the stool up to the sink and washed up the breakfast things then got the duster and wiped over the TV and the coffee table. I got the sweeper out and did the floors. When I finished I woke Mother with a cup of tea. She got out of bed, got dressed and prepared tea for Dave coming home. He was none the wiser. It went on like this for several weeks. I went to school and Mother got her sleep.

One morning, however, I went into my room to get

dressed and fell back asleep. I woke to screaming. It was Mother.

'Get your lazy arse out of bed!' she was yelling. I looked at the clock. It was 3.30 p.m. The day had gone. I couldn't believe I'd slept that long. I jumped up, did my chores and, when Dave came home, lied to him about what I'd done in school that day.

Two months on, I found Mother and Dave getting dressed in their fancy clothes. It could only mean one thing. They were going out tonight – together. My heart began pounding with an intensity that was now alarmingly familiar.

'Please don't send me to June's,' I cried. Mother just laughed.

'What are you making a fuss for? You're staying here,' she said.

What a relief. If someone was coming to the flat it would most likely be June, or Sue. Mother and Dave were soon ready to leave but were waiting for the sitter to turn up. I was so excited.

When the knock on the door came, I could barely contain myself. I stood behind Mum, butterflies in my stomach, waiting to see who it was. Then my blood went cold.

It wasn't June or Sue.

It was Adam.

4

I screamed. God, I screamed as though my lungs would burst. Mother erupted, slapping me hard around the back of the head.

'Get to your bed,' she said.

Gladly. I'd never run so fast. In my room I was safe. No one was allowed in there – the one benefit of having a deprived childhood. Mother and Dave were the only ones allowed. Even Stephanie, when she came over to play, wasn't permitted. Mother said it was because my room was a mess but the truth was I had no toys to play with.

By the age of six I had no concept of birthdays or Christmas. Not for me the nervous excitement of stepping into the lounge on Christmas morning. The whole Santa Claus thing was a mystery to me. During those early years he definitely never visited me.

In my room, I listened as Mother and Dave shouted 'Goodnight.'

The door closed. They were gone. Everything was silent and dark. My bed faced the door, which was slightly ajar. My eyes started to feel heavy but as I began to drift off the light from the hallway suddenly lit up my room. I looked up and, standing there, was Adam. My heart started to thump again; my breathing became faster. I closed my eyes and pretended to sleep. My blankets were being tugged but I gripped on to them so tightly I thought my fingers were going to be ripped off when he yanked the bedding away.

'Do you want to get up and watch the TV?' he said.

I opened my eyes and nodded my head. Dutifully, I got up and slowly walked down the hallway. All sorts of thoughts were going through my mind. What if Mother came back and copped me out of bed? What time was I allowed to stay up until? Was Adam going to hurt me again?

Adam followed me as I walked into the lounge. I sat on the armchair, looking around for some sort of comfort. I grabbed the cushion and held it tightly next to me, squeezing it so hard the filling went all out of shape.

'What you doing?' he said. 'If you wanna get up you have to sit next to me.'

He leered over me, hands behind his back, his glasses falling over the bridge of his nose so that he had to push them back with his finger.

'I want to go back to bed,' I said. I didn't want to sit next to him. The last time I did that he hurt me.

I tried to run back to my bedroom. I ran around him and headed towards the door, but he jumped over the sofa and banged the door shut. He stood over me. I could feel his breath on my face, but he was gulping like he was struggling for air. His breath smelled of stagnant water. My mouth filled with water too. I was going to be sick. I tried to push past him but he was so much bigger than me it was nearly impossible.

I suddenly felt very wet and sore, but warm. I looked down. I had wet myself. Adam stood over me, his long, greasy blond hair falling around his face. He looked at me and grinned. 'Now I have to clean you,' he said.

He took me to the bathroom and stripped me off. I was shaking so badly my teeth rattled together. Adam 'cleaned' me, using soap, nothing else, and I cried, while the whole time he had this permanent grin locked on his face.

When I was 'clean' he took me back to my bedroom. I got out clean nightwear from my drawer and got dressed, while he continued to watch me with his grin. I slipped back into bed and he kissed my cheek. With that, he left the room.

This ordeal became a regular occurrence. Each time was worse than the time before. Although he never once penetrated me, the touch of his body next to mine still hurt. I felt violated. Even though I was only six years old, I was no longer a little girl. Each time Mother went out, Adam would spend the evening in my room. I was touched, kissed, licked and bitten in places that I knew was wrong, but I was too scared to tell anyone.

'Your mum will have you put in care,' he told me. 'Dave will leave her and she will blame you for everything.' It was very confusing. Although I had happy memories of being with a foster family, now that I had been living with Mum for a while, the idea of being in care permanently scared me.

Soon I couldn't sleep at night and I got so tired I started falling asleep at school. Once, my teacher sent me to the head's office. He asked me why I was so tired. I said I wasn't but he made me lie on a camp bed in the reception area. I didn't go back to sleep, just lay there watching people come in and out, the children taking messages to other classes for their teachers. Everyone stopped to stare at me. When the bell went they let me go home.

I dreaded Mother going out but even when she stayed in I couldn't sleep. When I did drop off, through sheer exhaustion, I started to have night terrors, and to wet the bed. I'd dream people were flying up to my window, faces against the glass like they were watching me, calling me. I'd hide under the covers, shaking fiercely, so much so I'd lose control of my bladder. Mother took me to the doctor, who gave me medicine to control my bed-wetting. I'd heave at the sight of it and always gagged when I swallowed it. If I spilled any, Mother would give me another dose and give me a slap for getting medicine on the floor. She made fun of me for wetting the bed and told anyone who came round, including Stephanie, my only friend.

It got so bad that, one evening, I convinced myself I had to tell Mother. They were going out so often I couldn't cope any more. As they got ready to leave I started crying and begged Mother not to go out. She grabbed one of Dave's slippers, a soft shoe but with a deceptively hard sole. She slapped my bottom with it.

I yelped – a combination of pain and fear. The glint in her eye told me that the slipper had had the desired effect. Little did I know then that it would soon become Mother's weapon of choice. She dragged me off to bed. I screamed so hard I started coughing, my throat grew sore and I was red in the face.

Mother flung the door open, grabbed my hair and started shaking my head back and forth. She gave me one last slap in the mouth, and then she was gone. I could taste the blood in my mouth and was left with just the deafening silence in the room.

Suddenly, the door opened. I started screaming as loud as I could. My throat was agony, but I didn't care. Someone had to hear me and save me.

'You must go to sleep now,' Adam said.

I carried on screaming. Then I started swearing: 'Hate you, you bastard! Die!'

He left the room, closing the door behind him. Had he stopped? Had he finally realized what he was doing was wrong? Had my screaming worked?

The door flew open and there stood Mother, holding the slipper above her head. She rained about five blows to my quilt-covered body. I stopped screaming and stopped crying. Mother and Dave then left for their night out.

When he came back to my room, Adam didn't even have to say anything. The smarmy grin said it all. I just lay there. What else could I do?

During this time Mother's pregnancy was progressing and when my brother Alan was born in 1984, it was like the three of them sealed themselves up into a little unit. Even though I was outside it all, Mother still wanted me to call Dave 'Dad' and made no bones about telling me off if I didn't. I had to pretend to Dave it was all my idea and I wanted him to be my dad.

My other relatives loved my new 'father'; they thought he was the best thing since sliced bread. I suppose he was – at least compared to some of the other men Mother used to bring home. Mother loved him too, everyone could see that, and my baby brother was seen as the perfect gift for Mother and Dave. It was the start of a new life for them together, and I was left out. I was only a part of Mother's old life.

I didn't really care, though. For the most part, I was happy to be on my own. I was certainly used to it. I was on my own at school, I played on my own at home and, unless I was allowed to play out with Stephanie, I'd even be on my own when we visited Nan and Grand-dad. I was always the odd one out in our family because of my brown skin and because my mother always caused trouble. My older cousins would laugh at me and run off whenever I tried to play with them. All the girls played together and the boys did the same. I'd play in my nan's pantry, pretending to work in a supermarket. My nan even bought me a brown baby doll. I think she meant well but it just added to the overwhelming feeling I had that I was different.

It was only after Alan was born that I discovered the concept of birthdays and Christmas. Until then, I didn't even know my own birth date. Having birthday cards and presents was such a new thing in our house I thought the Queen had made some kind of declaration that year to make every parent do it. Back then, I thought the Queen decided everything.

When my brother was six months old, Adam's sister, Donna, began babysitting for us now and then. She and Mother seemed to get along so, when Donna was having difficulties with her own mum, she and her boyfriend, Richard, the fireman, moved in with us. He came to the house for the first time while I was in bed. The following morning I walked into the lounge to see a face that was covered in blood and badly bruised eyes. Donna said he had been jumped and they were mugged. Despite this rather scary introduction, Richard was really nice, very calm and softly spoken. Donna adored him.

They took my room while I shared with my brother, but I'd spend many hours lying on the bed while Donna brushed my hair and sang songs to me. I often wished Donna were my mum. She was beautiful, with long brown hair and the biggest brown eyes I'd ever seen, and she always wore the nicest clothes and smelled really sweet.

With Donna and Richard living with us, my parents thought it would be best for them to babysit us when they went out. I was ecstatic. I clung on to Donna's neck and didn't want to let go. My nightmare with Adam was over. She had saved me and she didn't even know it.

Things were going great. Donna would take me to school and collect me. Whenever she and Richard went out they took me, even to visit their friends. The only place I wouldn't go was to Donna's mother's house, because Adam was there.

Even though I was only young, I think I had a bit of a crush on Richard, possibly because he was the only man in my life who didn't want to hurt me. I'd often hear him and Donna talking about my parents. Donna wanted to leave, but Richard told her to wait.

One night while she was looking after me, she put on the video of 'Thriller', by Michael Jackson. The zombies and monsters in the film reminded me of my nightmares and I screamed and ran behind the sofa. Donna switched it off and explained that it wasn't real, just make-up and fake blood. I didn't care. I wasn't listening and didn't want to watch it, so she left it off.

For the first time in my life I felt truly happy. I should have known it wouldn't last. Mother had such a jealous streak she would accuse anyone and everyone of being after my dad. She saw Donna as competition, and she had to go.

One evening, it all kicked off. I hid in the corner of my room. I was convinced that if Donna left then Adam would come back. There was lots of shouting and slamming doors. After a while Donna and Richard came into my room to pack up their things.

'Can I come?' I pleaded with them. 'I'll be good. Please?'

They looked at each other and smiled. Then they each kissed my head and left.

Once again, I was on my own with Mother.

5

I was scratching around in the dirt, my scrapings becoming more and more frantic. Where was it? Where was the blessed money?

It had to be here somewhere. If I didn't find it I would be in big trouble.

I had retraced my steps, all the way to the shop and back, but it was nowhere to be seen. How could it have just vanished?

I thought of Mother's face, contorted in anger. She rarely needed an excuse to beat me, but this would do it, I knew that for sure.

My crime? I'd lost a ten-pence piece on the way back from the shop. Dad usually gave me the right money. If he didn't, he demanded I bring back the correct change and a receipt. I hadn't even realized anything was wrong until I got back to the house.

'Oi!' he'd said, in the menacing tone that instantly chilled my blood.

'What's she done now?' Mother said, appearing at his shoulder. Together they resembled some sort of two-headed monster.

'Nicked our money.'

'No, I didn't,' I said. 'I must have lost it on the way back.'

'Well?' Dad said. 'Go back and look for it.'

So that's what I'd done. Gone back to the shop, retracing every step, scanning the ground, looking for anything that might have resembled a silver coin. The ground had seemed awash with them but each time I stooped to pick one up it turned out it was a bottle top or foil wrapping. I had been right back to the shop and now I was on my hands and knees, tears streaming down my face, sifting through the dry mud of a puddle on the path. It was the only place it could be. Please, I prayed to anyone listening. Please let me find it. I could picture the slipper, raised high; could already feel its stinging burn on my arm.

'What are you doing, Collette?'

I looked up, shocked.

It was Sue, Stephanie's mum. She looked concerned.

'Looking for a 10p I lost,' I said. 'It's here some-where. I know it is.'

She went into her purse and pulled out a coin.

'Here you go,' she said kindly. 'Come on, I'll walk you home.'

I was so grateful I couldn't speak. She dried my eyes and walked home with me. Neither my mum nor my dad asked me where I found the coin. I don't think they really cared. They probably just wanted me out of the house for a while.

Stephanie's parents didn't make her hunt for lost change. They let her keep anything that was left over from trips to the shop. And she got pocket money for helping with chores in her house, like polishing or washing up.

I found this really strange. Mother never gave me money when I cleaned. Stephanie didn't even have to do it, whereas I did. I was never allowed out until my tasks were done.

To me, Stephanie had the perfect life. She always had the best trainers and clothes and she always had money to go to the shop. She was allowed to cross the road to play with kids from the other blocks and to go to the park up the road. I wasn't. Often I would sit on the kerb waiting for Stephanie to come back.

Although we went to different schools, I loved the stories Stephanie would tell me about her friends: who they were, the games she played with them and even what they wore to school.

At least I got to play a lot more with Stephanie. We each had a pair of roller skates and we would ride around the green pretending we were on horses or that we were police officers. Sometimes we would just walk around the green talking or singing. One day, we were larking about, singing 'Frankie' by Sister Sledge and a man walking by said we had such beautiful voices – like angels. He gave us a pound each. We ran to the shop and bought so many sweets, gorging on them, that we felt sick afterwards.

Now Donna and Richard had gone, I was apprehensive about who my new babysitter was going to be.

The next time they went out I waited on the sofa,

looking through the crack in the door to see who arrived. My heart was beating so fast it was like the sound of waves in my ears. It was a man named Simon, one of Dad's new friends. He and his wife lived down the road and had their own house. They had children, but I never played with them. Mother often went to bingo with Simon's wife. She would look at me funny, she never smiled or said hello and, in fact, I couldn't recall her ever speaking to me at all.

As my parents went out they said I was allowed to stay up. Simon let me watch a sitcom called *Me and My Girl*. I loved it. Then he made tea and toast and we both sat on the sofa, watching television. After a while I brushed my teeth and went to bed. When I was tucked up he stuck his head around the door, said goodnight and then left.

So it went on. I started to like it when he came to babysit. Another programme I enjoyed was *Blankety Blank*. When it was time to go to bed I went without any fuss and began to sleep once more without the fear of waking up.

One evening I started speaking to Simon about his children, asking the same curious questions any child would: what were their names, how old were they, what school did they go to. Then I asked: 'Have they been touched?'

Simon looked at me, mouth open. Something was stopping him from speaking. He stood up and switched off the TV.

Suddenly I realized what I'd said. I wanted to take it back but didn't know how.

'I want to go to bed,' I said, covering my ears with my hands. I didn't want to talk about it now. I didn't want anyone to know. It had stopped now, after all. Why the hell did I ask that question?

'Who did this, babe?' he said.

At first I couldn't speak, it was like I had a stone in my throat. I couldn't even swallow. I went into a cold sweat. My stomach was churning.

'Please don't tell Mum or Dad,' I said. I didn't want to be taken away. I remembered what Adam had said. If Dave left, Mother would hate me. By then it was early 1985, I was seven, Mother was pregnant again and they were talking about moving house and, now that she was divorced from Steve, even getting married. I didn't want to miss any of that.

I told Simon everything – when it started, when it finished, about Donna and Richard and how nice he was for letting me stay up to watch programmes without 'paying the consequences'. He smiled at me, then got up and went into the kitchen. I sat on the sofa feeling strangely light. It was so good to tell someone. I hadn't told Stephanie. She wouldn't have wanted to be my friend if she knew. Things like that only happened to dirty girls – that's what was said about abuse back then. It was such a taboo. Being a child of the early eighties, there wasn't anyone to speak to without them telling your parents. And that was the last thing I wanted to happen.

Simon came back with tea and toast. He switched on the television, never once saying a word. We ate and drank in silence. When I'd finished I curled into the corner of the sofa, nightdress pulled over my knees. Simon got up and switched off the light. This was the norm. We were just sitting, watching TV before my bedtime. Then I felt a finger rubbing my ankle. I looked over, and Simon was staring at me.

He moved his hand and put his arm around my shoulders. He pulled me towards him, stroking my hair, kissing the top of my head. I tried to pull away.

'I'm not like him. I won't hurt you,' he said. 'And you're a special little girl.'

I relaxed. I believed him. He carried on holding me when it was time for my bed.

'Stay up a bit later,' he said. 'I won't tell 'cause I'll get into trouble.'

I wanted to stay up, but my eyes were so heavy. I could feel him fiddling with the cushions before he laid my head down. He pulled my legs out straight so I was lying down on the sofa. Simon jumped over me so he was lying behind. He continued to hold me as I began to fall asleep.

I don't know how long I was sleeping but, suddenly, I jumped. Something wasn't right. Simon's hand was between my legs, inside my pants, 'cupping' me. I jumped up and ran to the bathroom. He ran after me.

'You want to hurt me too,' I said.

'No, no,' he said pleadingly. 'He didn't love you. That's why it hurt. This doesn't hurt, does it?'

It didn't hurt, but it also didn't feel right. Was I being stupid? Is this how people loved each other? Was I being oversensitive? Surely he didn't want to hurt me. He had children of his own and he seemed to love me like his own kids.

When my parents came home, nothing was said. Simon became the permanent sitter, and on nights he came round I would allow him to lie next to me on the sofa with his hands in my underwear. He never once hurt me, but I felt so uncomfortable. I didn't tell him this because he told me that he was my parents' last option.

'If I don't babysit you, then Adam will be back,' he said.

That was enough for me to let him touch me. I would rather that than have the most disgusting things done to me by a person who gained pleasure out of seeing me shamed and beaten.

One day, my parents took me with them when they went to Simon's house. It was so noisy, with kids running in and out of rooms, screaming and laughing, having fun. My mother pushed me towards them. I held back and she pinched my arm and shoved me. The other kids stopped and stared at me. I could feel my face burning up as I fought back tears.

'Don't you dare show me up!' Mother spat.

I walked slowly towards the kitchen. Kids pushed past me and ran out the back door. I went out and sat on the step. There were two boys and two girls, all playing Stuck in the Mud. I giggled as they ducked and dived, running to the wall, calling 'Den!' just so they could catch their breath. But not one of them asked me to play. I was sitting there wishing they would, but the only thing I got was the odd glance now and then. When the other kids ran back into the house I made the brave move of following them inside. They went upstairs but, as they'd not asked me to join in, I knew I couldn't follow them.

I sneaked into the lounge and sat on a chair. No one noticed me come in. The adults were all talking and throwing their heads back with laughter. Mother followed Simon's wife into the kitchen to make a drink. My brother needed his nappy changed so Dad took him to the bathroom.

I looked at Simon and he winked at me. I smiled as he asked me questions about school.

'You're still a special little girl,' he said.

With that I jumped up and went to sit on his lap. I had my arms wrapped around his neck when his wife came in.

'What the fuck is your daughter doing?' she shouted.

My mother was walking in behind her. Mother grabbed me by my hair and pulled me off Simon's lap.

'Dirty little bitch,' she said.

I was confused. It was only a cuddle. It probably

wasn't 'normal', but I was never told any different and my parents didn't want to question it – well, Mother didn't. When Dad came back from changing my brother the room fell silent.

'I want to go home,' Mother said. 'Right now.'

Dad didn't ask why. He got my brother settled in his pushchair and we left. I never saw Simon after that.

That at least signalled an end to the sexual assaults – for the time being, anyway – but I wasn't out of the woods yet. More misery was lurking just around the corner.

6

In June 1985, Mother gave birth to a little girl, Audrey. If Alan's birth had signalled a sizeable shift in attention away from me, then the arrival of my little sister made it even more obvious. In the eyes of Mother and my dad, the four of them now made an even more perfect little unit – and, again, I didn't always feel a part of it. Audrey's birth led to another significant change. When she was two, Mother announced we were all packing up. We were moving to a house, which meant a bigger room for me and a garden of our own.

I was so excited. Mother said it was a new start for all of us. As I got into the car and waved goodbye to Stephanie I remember thinking: My parents do love me. They're taking me with them, so they must love me.

I was nine when we moved, and I loved our new house in Perry Common, just four miles away. It had an upstairs and my brother and I would slide down the stairs on our bottoms. Just like our flat, it had three bedrooms, but it was much bigger. I shared a bedroom with my sister.

Although the house was bigger, at first it wasn't very nice to live in. Mum and Dad had brought the carpets from the flat with them, but they didn't fit the floors and never had grippers, so the edges were frayed with the boards beneath showing. We had garish, red velvet furniture, with cigarette burns all over it.

In time, Dad got round to redecorating and my sister got to choose the wallpaper, because she was the youngest. She was mad about Care Bears at the time, so we had the wallpaper and quilt covers. It was a bit babyish for me but at least we had a proper house with a big back garden, so I didn't care.

The kitchen was quite small, as was Mother's pantry and a bathroom that led off it. One major drawback was that the toilet was outside. It was horrible when it rained or snowed. Rain would come under the toilet door, soaking my slippers. Even if this happened, I would have to keep them on. I wasn't allowed to walk around barefoot or with just socks on. If either Mum or Dad caught me they made me wear the same socks the following day. This would be embarrassing if it coincided with gym class at school. Dad said it was to show that I appreciated my mother doing my washing. Dad eventually knocked the pantry and bathroom out so mother had a bigger kitchen. She had a huge pine dining-room table with chairs to match.

The best thing about our new home was that we had our own back garden, and it was enormous, with an apple and a pear tree and a big conifer stuck in the middle of the grass. There was a raised bedding area with wild flowers. Our neighbours were elderly and they filled my parents in on the previous tenant. They showed us pictures of our garden and it had been beautiful. It had won awards for Best Garden in Birmingham, but, of course, my parents didn't care. The garden soon became a dumping ground for rubbish and bits of broken wood, and the raised bedding area became a site for bonfires. The only interest my parents took in the garden was my dad's vegetable patch.

One thing I noticed about our move was that I no longer seemed to see Penny, the social worker. She stopped coming round. I didn't really think much of it at the time but, now that I do, no one really came round to check on us. It was like they were leaving us alone.

Not long after we moved to our new house I had to go into hospital to have my tonsils taken out. Dad took me on the morning of my surgery. He carried my overnight bag for me and, when we got to the ward, the nurse showed me to my bed.

I had been there half an hour when he said he had to leave. He left me sitting in a gown on the edge of my bed waiting for the surgeon to come and get me. The later it got, the more scared I became. I watched as the lift doors opened and a surgeon wearing his mask pushed a bed out to collect the next patient. My nerves got the better of me and I went to ask the nurse when it was my turn. She had a list in front of her.

As I got to the desk the lift door opened again and out stepped another surgeon with a bed. He stood at the end of the ward and called my name. I stood by the desk and screamed. The nurse jumped up and ran over to me.

'I don't want to go,' I said. 'The people in the masks scare me.'

She knelt down beside me and hugged me.

'Don't worry,' she said. 'I'll come with you to the theatre and I can stay with you till it's over.'

I wiped away my tears and went with her and the surgeon. I didn't want to go on the bed, so they let me walk. When we got to the theatre the nurse pulled me up on to her lap and started talking to me about school. She told me to count to ten and it would all be over. I don't know what I counted up to, but I know I didn't get to ten.

I woke up back on the ward in my bed. My throat was sore and I had a really bad headache. I looked around and could see the other kids from the ward walking about, getting toys from the day room. Parents were sitting by their bedsides with concerned looks on their faces. They hugged their children, patted them, said encouraging things to them. I longed to have parents like that, or even someone like the kindly Penny, my old social worker. At least I felt she cared about me.

My parents weren't there. They had said they would be coming in the evening after they had dinner. In the hospital I had my dinner, with jelly and ice cream for pudding. This was a real treat. I didn't have puddings at home and I loved ice cream.

When evening came, Mother didn't come to visit me but Dad did. He said she had to stay home to look after my brother and sister. He didn't really speak to me, but he did ask how I was feeling.

When I told him the nurse had come to the theatre with me because I was scared he shouted at me for wasting her time.

'You're a big tit,' he said. 'Sitting on the nurse's lap. You've embarrassed me. If I'd known you were going to play up I would've hung around. You wouldn't have pissed about if I'd been here.'

When he had finished having a go at me he read the newspaper and didn't look up again until the bell rang for the end of visiting time. He picked me up the next morning to take me home. Mother sent me to bed for three days. I was only allowed to get up to go to the toilet or to have dinner. It was worse than hospital.

I had no TV or radio, just books. I wasn't allowed to lie on the sofa because I 'would take up too much room'. In my room, I was out of sight, out of mind. It was easy for them to forget about me.

When I was well again, it didn't take long for Mother's persecution of me to begin in earnest.

Some of the beatings I received I can find a reason for. Knocking over drinks, breaking plates – these were things for which she would beat me. I probably was clumsy, not that children should be hit for such things.

Sometimes, however, I was genuinely mystified. One day, Mother wanting my brother's bedroom redecorated, I was helping her strip the old paper off the walls. With UB40 blasting on the stereo and the windows wide open, with the sun blazing in, I was having fun. I was getting lost in the words of the song 'Red, Red Wine'.

BANG!

I turned on my heels to find my sister lying on the floor. She just lay there with Mother, my brother and me looking over her. She started to laugh and held on to her arm. Then I looked again. Her arm was the wrong way round.

I screamed, pointing to it. Mother belted me across the face and spat: 'This is your fault.'

She scooped up Audrey and ran down the stairs. I followed, my brother behind me. Mother was dialling 999. She looked so pale and frightened that I started to panic too. My face was still stinging from the slap but I knelt next to my sister. She was lying on the sofa while Mother was on the phone.

After she had hung up, she picked up the phone again and called Dad. I sat and stared straight through her as she stood there telling him what had happened.

'Col just pushed her.'

My mind rewound three minutes to when it happened. Had I pushed her? No. Had I knocked her without knowing? Maybe. If that did happen, then surely it was an accident? But no, I know it didn't happen that way. For a start, my sister had been on the opposite side of the room to me. It was impossible.

I believe the reason she fell was because Mother

allowed her to stand on the speaker. She lost her balance, fell and broke her arm. It was an accident.

Mother took my brother with her when my sister left in the ambulance. She left me at home, waiting for them all to get back, to get the blame for what had happened.

I was sitting in the armchair watching TV, nervously biting my nails and thinking about how I was going to tell Dad the truth about what had happened. I had a cold feeling, with my heart in my throat. I was innocent, yet I felt so guilty.

Then I heard it.

The sound of the engine getting louder as the car got closer to the house. Then I heard the car pulling up the kerb on to the drive. I started shaking. I ran into the kitchen and put the kettle on. The key was in the door.

I froze in the kitchen doorway. As the front door opened I ran back into the kitchen and started getting the cups out of the cupboard. As I stood I felt a burn across my ear and my head smacked off the wall.

I looked up and there was Dad, the slipper in his hand. I ran around the table, catching my slippers on the chairs, which caused me to stall.

I ran through to the lounge, where Mother grabbed me and threw me on to the chair. She grabbed the slipper off Dad and smacked my backside so hard I actually screamed. I ran up the stairs like a scolded puppy.

I cried so hard, not just because of the pain but

because I knew that this was wrong. The beating was so bad I had swollen marks on my skin from the slipper.

I slept on my stomach all night.

I couldn't understand what I'd done wrong. Did Mother hate me? Did she blame me for her life turning out a certain way? I didn't know and, certainly, then, I was too young to understand. All I knew was how unfair it felt.

When I started at my new school I made friends almost straight away with a girl named Abbie who lived only a few doors down from me on the green. We'd often play after school, once I had completed my chores, of course. With her three sisters we'd play Tag or Hide and Seek. In school we were inseparable. She confided that she had problems at home too. Her dad was an alcoholic, so we would often sit on the concrete posts talking about how unfair our parents were and what slaps they had dished out the night before. It felt good knowing I finally had someone to talk to, although I never told her everything.

I started to think things might not be so bad after all.

Then one night I did something that upset Mother. I can't even remember what sparked it now, but she suddenly erupted.

She grabbed me and swung me round the lounge by my hair then threw me up against the wall. I fell to the ground and she laid into me, slapping me round the head, spit coming from her mouth as she launched into a barrage of names and obscenities. It ended with me running up the stairs and jumping into my bed, pulling the quilt up for protection and listening for what was coming next. It stayed silent. She hadn't followed me. Even though it was only 4 p.m. I fell asleep until next morning.

That day I got up as usual, had my breakfast, got dressed and went to school. I walked slowly past Abbie's house so she could see me. Dad said I wasn't allowed to call for her on the way. I'd talk too much and be late. However, Abbie saw me and came running. I looked back and there was Dad watching, making sure I went straight to school.

When we got into the playground I told her what Mother had done the night before. Abbie put her arm around me, and I cried. We didn't talk about it for the rest of the day. We both knew that, no matter what, we would always be friends and no one else would know about our parents.

Later that day, the headteacher, Miss Hardwick, called me to her office. She had a reputation for being very strict. If you were naughty you had to stand in the corner with a finger on your lips. When I got called in I thought: What have I done?

Miss Hardwick was very stern-faced. She was an older lady, not that tall, with long, dark hair. She had a massive office, with a sofa and chairs and a desk at the back. When I entered there was a smell of coffee.

She sat me on the sofa.

'How are you getting on, Collette?' she said.

'OK,' I said.

'Do you miss your old school?'

I shrugged.

'How are your parents?' she asked.

'Why are you asking me that?' I said.

She took hold of my arm and lifted up my jumper. I had bruises from the beating Mother had given me the night before.

'Sometimes Mother gets very angry,' I said. 'But it's OK. I'm used to it.'

Then a strange thing happened. She got up and left the room. I was on my own in the office for ages. I didn't know what to do. Was I to stay there? Should I go back to class?

Eventually, just as I had stood up and got ready to leave, the door opened. Miss Hardwick walked in, followed by a lady dressed in a skirt and blouse. The headteacher told me this was a social worker.

'Can you tell her everything you told me ... and Abbie?' Miss Hardwick said.

By then I already suspected that Abbie had told someone.

I thought about what to do. Here was a teacher urging me to tell a social worker what I went through at home. I thought of Penny. Social workers were there to help, weren't they? Yet she had left me with Mother. Maybe I couldn't trust them to sort this out. And, after it all, I had to face Mother and Dad.

I decided to speak. I told the woman about life at home, how I felt like an outsider, how Mother often erupted in rage, mostly for no reason.

She sat and listened. There was sorrow on her face, but she didn't say much.

Afterwards, a doctor examined me and Abbie was also questioned.

I had spent most of the day in the office and now the bell was ringing, signifying home time. I had to go. Mother would be waiting for me. I had to be in the house within ten minutes of school finishing or I would be sent to bed early. I tried to leave, but Miss Hardwick stood in front of the door.

'Your parents are coming,' she said. 'We need to sort this out before you go home.'

I sat and stared out of the window, watching all the other children running out of the school gates, excited to go home and play. I so wanted to be out there with them. I knew Mother and Dad were going to be angry. I had opened my mouth about what Mother had done to me, and I would definitely be punished now.

I watched as they walked down the path into the school reception. I could tell by the look on their faces that they were angry. Miss Hardwick called them into her office and sent me to the waiting area with the school secretary while the social worker and the head-teacher talked with them. As I walked past my parents, they gave me 'the look'. My heart was racing, my mouth drier than sand.

Sitting in the large, comfy chair, I started to think what I could tell my parents.

I'll lie and say I never said anything, pretend I don't know what's going on, but then again, I might be taken away. I'll tell the social workers that I want to go back to my old home and live with Stephanie.

After what seemed like an age, they called me back into Miss Hardwick's office. Greeting me were more dirty looks from my parents. Mother looked like she'd been crying. No one spoke to me.

The adults spoke among themselves for a few minutes. Then we were allowed home. As the school door shut behind me I knew that another beating was waiting for me and it would be bed with no dinner again.

The next day my parents removed me from that school and sent me to another.

'I'm not having anyone tell me how to be a parent,' Dad said.

And that was it. The incident was never mentioned again in our house. For a few weeks afterwards I waited for the repercussions. Surely my old school would report to social services that I had been removed. Surely the social worker who attended that day would follow it up. But there was nothing. It was like I didn't exist. I'd fallen through the cracks. Was there anyone anywhere looking out for me?

7

The first I became aware something was up was when Mother came upstairs.

'Where's your sister?' she said.

'I don't know,' I said. 'I thought she was downstairs with you.'

I was sitting in my room reading. Audrey had wanted to play but I told her I just wanted to sit with my book. She wasn't playing with Alan, nor was she in our parents' room. There was no sign of her downstairs and the front door was open. She was missing.

After a mild panic Mother discovered she was at a friend's house three doors down. Audrey had taken herself off there without telling anyone where she was going.

By the time Mother called my dad, it was spun that Audrey had run away because I'd told her she wasn't wanted. It was complete lies, concocted to cover Mother's shortcomings.

When, not long after, Alan fell and cut his nose open on a brick playing wheelbarrows, Mother blamed me – even though I was inside the house at the time. When Audrey cut her hair, it was my fault, even though I was at school.

If my brother or sister dropped food on the floor,

Mother made me pick it up. My brother would kick me under the table, but if I kicked back or told Mother she would send me outside to eat the rest of my dinner. Even if it was raining, which it was on many occasions, she'd order me outside. My food would swim in rainwater until I had to tilt the plate to get rid of the puddles.

If the weather was warm I could at least sit and listen to the birds in the trees, smell the summer air and dream about being far away. The garden table was by the back gate, so I could hear the kids in the street riding up and down on their bikes or playing Kerby.

When the weather turned cold I had to pull my jumper over my hands and try to cut my food without it flying off my plate. Sometimes it would be so cold that I couldn't cut it. Regardless, I had to eat it.

'You can either eat it or starve,' Mother said. 'Your choice.'

One evening, Alan complained I was kicking him. Mother was in a foul mood anyway. Without a word she picked up the bottle of tomato ketchup and tipped it over my head. Sauce dripped from my hair down to my face. My siblings and she were in hysterics. My clothes were covered. I moved to go and clean myself up.

'Stay where you are,' Mother said, crying with laughter. I had to stay and eat my dinner before she allowed me to leave.

Even aside from humiliating episodes like that, dinner times were the worst. I had to prepare the table, help with the cooking, wash and dry up and clean the floor. Some of the food Mother cooked I didn't like, but I had to eat it. I hated liver and onions but if I voiced an opinion she would send me outside with it or leave me with nothing at all.

You might think being outside would have been better. I could throw the food away there, perhaps? Mother was wise to that. She and Dad would take it in turns to watch me out of the window, so I'd mix the food with my mash potato and swallow without chewing. I'd gag but they wouldn't let me have a drink. I had to make cups of tea at dinnertime and that would be our mealtime drink, but we were only allowed it once we had finished our food.

I became the scapegoat for everyone, not just Mother. My siblings soon woke up to the fact that if they broke anything or hurt each other they could tell Mother I did it.

It was my job to make sure their beds were made, the bedrooms were tidy and they were dressed in the mornings. From the age of eight my bedtime was usually the same, 6 p.m., because there was always something I hadn't done properly or my siblings had grassed on me for some reason or another.

If they were in a good mood, bedtime was eight o'clock. Mother took us to bed, so we would take it in turns to kiss Dad goodnight and go to the toilet. Then we had to run up the stairs and get straight into bed because Mother didn't like any messing about. She had things to watch on TV.

As I ran up the stairs I'd cross my fingers and say three times: 'Please don't tell me off, please don't tell me off, please don't tell me off.'

Every night I did this because, invariably, if I didn't, I'd get shouted at for something. Mother would always check under my bed at bedtimes to make sure I didn't have any books or bottles of water under there. We had no TV either and bedtimes were for sleep only.

Mother would sit on the stairs and listen. If I coughed or breathed heavily she would storm in and accuse me of still being awake.

'You're not breathing as if you're asleep,' she'd say. And I'd get a slap for not being asleep.

Summertime was the worst. Whether it was 6 p.m. or 8 p.m., it would still be bright outside. I used to sneak a book into bed and, while reading, I'd listen for the creaks on the stairs. When I heard one I knew she was listening so I'd throw my book down the side of my bed and pull the bed covers over my head. Sometimes I'd get caught with the book and sometimes my sister would grass on me.

The beatings didn't hurt any more. I knew to cover my head and face, as those were the places that stung the most.

Although Abbie and I had been at different schools for some time, I still saw her, and we played together now and again. Only after I left my previous school did I find out the circumstances that had led me to Miss Hardwick's office. Despite swearing not to tell a soul,

Abbie had been upset and confided in her class teacher. He had told the headteacher, who called me in. I tried to put the episode behind me – after all, Abbie had her own troubles with her alcoholic father – but I couldn't stop thinking that she had betrayed me.

However, because she knew what my mother was like, she was the only friend that I would invite to my house. I didn't feel too embarrassed if Mother scolded me in front of her. Our friendship wasn't to last much longer, though.

Not long afterwards, Abbie asked if she could stay over one night. I felt it was a bad idea, but she persisted. She thought we'd have this super-fun sleepover where we'd get up for a midnight feast and not sleep at all because we'd tell each other ghost stories. I knew otherwise.

My first surprise was when my parents said yes. I had expected a firm and stern no. When the weekend came we played out on our bikes for most of the Saturday. At teatime we sat at the table and ate our dinner. I felt slightly embarrassed asking my parents if I could leave the table in front of her, but I think she understood because she asked too. We washed up and went into the garden to play. I hadn't been shouted at all day and I was having so much fun.

Then it was time for bed. Abbie was allowed to bed later at weekends but in our house Saturday bedtime was eight o'clock. We lay in bed making shadows on the wall with our fingers, giggling and talking about school and our favourite soaps. We were whispering so no one could hear us, and I felt so naughty when I heard my parents go to bed and I was still awake. We soon got to the stage where we weren't even talking sense we were that tired.

Suddenly the door flew open and there stood Mother, practically foaming at the mouth. She pulled the quilt back and Abbie jumped out of bed. Mother rained down blow after blow, pulling me half out of the bed by my hair, all the time punching while I grabbed for the quilt.

I finally got the duvet and pulled it over my head.

'You dirty black lesbian,' she shouted. 'Go to sleep.'

She stopped hitting me.

'I've hurt my fucking hand now, 'cause of you!'

She punched me one more time then left.

Abbie slipped back into bed. We lay there with our backs to each other, shaking with fear. My head was hot and felt like it was bleeding, but it was stinging from where Mother had pulled a handful of hair out. My whole body was aching from the slaps and punches. We didn't speak. The same fear of Mother coming back was between us. I didn't know what time it was, but I know it was early morning when we both eventually fell asleep.

The next morning Abbie left before breakfast. She never told her parents what happened that night, nor anyone else. We didn't even speak to each other. The one friend I confided in had seen enough. She never called for me again. Our contact extended to an exchange of hellos to each other whenever we passed in the street.

It was horrible. I watched as Abbie rode past my house on her bike with her new friends. I felt jealous. We knew everything about each other, yet we never spoke. It was like a brick wall had been thrown up between us and other kids clued on to it. They started to make up stories about Abbie and me, saying we had each said things that we hadn't.

One day, after some kids had been causing trouble, winding me up about something Abbie had supposedly said about my dad, I saw her in the street. Instead of questioning her about it, I attacked her. I pushed her into a neighbour's garage and started punching and kicking her.

Abbie then started hanging out with a boyfriend, but he treated her terribly, dragging her up the street by her hair and punching her in front of everyone.

Another day, I was sitting on the steps outside my house with our neighbour's son, Jack, with the front door wide open. It was a warm day and my parents were out shopping, but I was feeling crap after another beating from them.

Abbie walked past the house. I made a comment to her about being a beaten girlfriend and what a mug she was for putting up with it. She stopped and glared, and then she ran for me. Jack got up and stood in the doorway. I told him to move, but Abbie pushed him to the side.

She went for my hair, but I managed to move and she fell on the bottom step. I grabbed her by the hair and pulled her up the steps, stopping just before the top. Jack slammed the front door shut and I battered Abbie's head off the steps. I couldn't stop.

It wasn't Abbie I was seeing, it was Mother. All the pent-up rage I felt at her I was taking out on Abbie. Jack pulled me off and Abbie curled up on the steps and started crying.

My hands shaking with adrenalin, I sat next to her. We were silent. I put my arm around her shoulder and said, 'Sorry.'

My head was spinning. This was once my best friend and here I was beating the crap out of her. Something wasn't right.

I was turning into my mother. Oh God, was this the fate mapped out for me? Was it inescapable? Thinking I could end up like her terrified me, yet still I couldn't help it. If there was any hint of people talking about my home life then I was going to fight.

These were things I had to deal with. I wasn't ready for finger-pointing or questions or nasty people's jibes. My home life was personal. It was a journey I was trying to get through.

The sexual assaults had stopped, for the moment at least, but along with the physical violence, I would soon be facing a new terror, and its effects were to be even longer-lasting – mental torture.

8

I could not stand it any longer. The discomfort was unbearable. I knew I'd be shouted at but, frankly, I didn't care. I had to go to the toilet.

It sounds extreme, because it was. Going to the toilet meant going downstairs. It meant being out of bed – a cardinal sin in my parents' eyes.

There had been times when I'd been so scared of their wrath, so petrified of going downstairs, that I'd started wetting the bed again. My memories of their teasing and laughing and that horrible medicine they'd forced me to take when I'd done it before were fresh in my mind. I'd told no one. In the morning, if I woke up to find the quilt soaked through, I'd make the bed to make it look like nothing was wrong. The next night I'd run up the stairs and wrap the quilt around me so the smell of urine didn't get out. My parents would come in and say goodnight, none the wiser that my eyes were streaming from the smell. As soon as I had a chance to change the covers I took it, emptying out Mother's wash basket and placing the dirty sheets at the bottom. I did it so many times it was a wonder I never got caught. So far, though, I never had.

This night was agony, however. I had to go

downstairs. By now the bathroom had been modernized. Dad had finally renovated the kitchen, knocking out the pantry and outdoor toilet and making the kitchen much bigger. The bathroom was now nice – he'd done a good job. But it meant the toilet was still downstairs.

I crept down and sat on the bottom step, trying to pluck up the courage to ask to go. I'd had an icky tummy all day and not long after I'd gone to bed I'd needed to go. I lightly knocked on the lounge door. Nothing.

The TV was on, but there was no other sound. I knocked again. Nothing.

'Mum?' I called. Nothing.

I slowly pushed the door open. Was this a trap? I peered around the door. There was no one there. I ran to the toilet, did what I needed to do and ran back upstairs. I lay there, heart pounding so loud it was coming through my ears. What should I do? Should I stay in bed? Should I go and tell the neighbours we were on our own?

I sat up. Why was the TV still on? Maybe they had gone to the shop. They'd be back in a minute. I settled back down. I don't know how long I lay there, but the next thing I knew Dad was calling me for school.

I didn't say anything to my parents about them going out. If they thought I knew, we would have another sitter, and that wasn't a risk I was willing to take. I'd rather have intruders break in and kill me than have another sitter. That was my view.

When we were put to bed early, even though I had been good, I knew my parents were going out again. I lay in bed listening to them whispering in their room while they got ready. They didn't put their shoes on until they were downstairs. I heard the lounge door close and the key being put in the front door to close it so as not to make a noise.

I waited for ten minutes then sneaked downstairs. There was a slipper behind the living-room door. Such an instrument of torture, it looked quite harmless lying there. Once in the living room, I was almost scared to touch anything in case they would know. I just watched some television and then went back upstairs.

I woke with a start. Someone was coming upstairs. It was Mother. Her face was red. In her hand was the slipper.

'This will teach you to go downstairs when we're out,' she spat between blows over the duvet.

How had she known?

Despite catching me out, my parents continued to sneak out. After that last beating it took me a long time before I ventured downstairs again but, one night, I decided to risk it. I opened the living-room door and saw the slipper. Then I realized. That's how they knew I had been up. They had left it behind the door so if it had moved they would know that someone had come down. I moved it to the side so I'd remember to put it back later. I watched the music channels until I got tired, then took myself back off to bed, making sure I put the slipper back so my parents wouldn't know.

What I loved about sneaking out of bed wasn't the TV. It was that I could go to the toilet. It was relief.

One night I had a biscuit, a digestive. Just one. Later I was in bed fast asleep when I heard banging on the stairs. It sounded like the house was being invaded. I shot up.

I'm going to die, I thought.

The door flew open, and there was Mother. She dragged me out of my bed. I was confused, wondering what the heck was going on. I still thought we were being invaded, even though I was in no doubt it was Mother dragging me down the stairs by my hair.

I fell to my knees halfway down, but she carried on pulling. As she got to the bottom I fell down, face forward towards the front door. Mother went on dragging me. She had such a tight grip. No matter which way I turned my head it burned.

Dad stood in the lounge in front of the fire. On the coffee table were two cups of tea and the packet of digestives.

'Thief!' Dad shouted.

'I haven't done anything,' I said, but I knew they knew. I had stolen a biscuit out of the cupboard.

'Lying bitch,' Mother said.

She gathered three or four of the digestives, grabbed my jaw and yanked it open. She was so forceful I gagged. Then she started shoving the biscuits into my mouth. I spat some out but she picked up the pieces and shoved them back in. I heaved and gagged. My throat was stinging from the dryness of the biscuits.

When she released her grip I turned and ran back up the stairs and into bed. She followed. I pulled the pillow over my head and wrapped the quilt around me. Blow after blow rained down. I felt like a punchbag.

'I'm sorry, I'm sorry,' I said, over and over.

When she felt I had been punished enough, she left the room.

I hated this house. I hated my parents. I wanted to leave home.

Knowing not to eat the food stuck in my mind each time my parents went out, but it was difficult. They had chocolate bars and crisps in the cupboard, along with cakes that Nan had brought that weekend, but everything was accounted for. I only had to have a slice of bread or cheese and they'd know. I still couldn't believe they knew about the digestive.

Sometimes at night I felt so hungry I thought I'd be sick, even though there was nothing in my tummy. Out of desperation I scoured the fridge and the kitchen cupboards looking for things I could eat without being detected. I took a teaspoonful of sugar and savoured the sweet grains on my tongue. Next I ate a chunk of butter. Sickly and salty it was, but it was food and I was so grateful I ate another lump.

On another night, I was worried that the butter was getting low so I peeled a potato. I didn't have time to cook it so I ate it raw. It was hard and crunchy and strangely tasteless, but I didn't care. Afterwards I got paranoid about the peelings. If I put them in the bin Mother would surely find them and then I'd get the slipper. I ran up the garden in the dark and buried them by Dad's vegetable plot. I simply couldn't leave any evidence.

On the nights I knew my parents were staying in I filled my dressing-gown pockets with toilet tissue and once in bed I hid under the covers and ate the tissue – anything to convince my body I was eating, to take away the hunger pains.

I wasn't allowed water in my room so, if I needed a drink, I had to be resourceful. I had a pocket water game which had a dolphin inside. You had to press the pump buttons to get the rings on the dolphin's nose. When my thirst became too much I drank the water from inside the game, sneaking it downstairs the following morning to refill it for the following night.

I would like to say that bedtime was the worst but, actually, it wasn't. During the day, when I had nothing to hide under, was the worst. The slaps and digs were much sharper, especially against bare skin.

For two years, it was endless, and the stress of wondering when Mother would kick off again was exhausting. When would this torture end?

9

When I was eleven it was time to leave junior school. Most of my friends from school and the kids who lived by me went to the secondary school that was only two minutes from my house. I assumed I would join them. My dad had other ideas.

It wasn't up to me to choose my school. It was out of my hands. Dad went to the open days and came back and said whether it was good enough or not. So the school I ended up going to was near my nan's house. Every morning, no matter the weather, I'd have to ride my bike the twenty minutes to my nan's. I'd prop it up outside her house underneath the bay window and walk up to school.

I made new friends in secondary. One of them was called Laura. I'd call in for her on the way to school and we'd walk up together, talking about the day ahead. We became really close. I'd tell her about my parents and she'd tell me about her dad and how he treated her mum. Her mum was very quiet, always smiling and very religious.

On weekends my parents allowed me to hang out at Laura's and we'd spend the whole morning cooking lunch. Once we made sausage and tomato sandwiches.

The bread was so soaked from the tomato juice that it fell apart when we tried to eat it. We laughed so hard.

We'd play Madonna and Whitney on the stereo. Laura had such a beautiful singing voice. I would sit there and pretend I was her audience while she danced and sang her heart out.

When her dad came home we would switch off the stereo and dive on to the sofa. Laura often stood up for herself where her father was concerned. I admired the fact that she wouldn't allow him to speak to her like she was nothing. If she didn't want to do something for him, she'd say so. I so wanted to be like her, and I told her so too.

She promised that if my parents were being nasty then I could stay at hers, but that was easier said than done. My dad was suspicious of my new friend, but I had a weapon up my sleeve. Dad fixed cars and was really into motors. Laura's dad owned a garage, and her mother mentioned my dad to him. Before long, Dad got a job there and in time he effectively ran the garage and was doing a job he loved. This made life much easier for Laura and me. I stayed at her house most weekends.

I was even allowed to give her my phone number, but I wasn't allowed to use the phone so if she wanted to speak to me she'd have to make the call. My parents had a block on the phone. To use it you had to punch in a code and of course I never knew the code. And when she called, she knew I couldn't talk, as my parents would turn down the TV and listen to my conversations.

I stayed at Laura's any opportunity I had. I didn't want to be at home. At least if I wasn't there I couldn't be blamed for anything.

If I stayed over, the deal was that I had to be home no later than ten o'clock on Sunday morning, because that was my cleaning day. Mother would prepare dinner and vacuum and polish downstairs while Dad went to the pub. My job was to strip the beds, vacuum and polish the bedrooms and put clean quilt covers and sheets on. It wasn't too bad doing my siblings' or my bed, but Mother's bed was huge and the quilt was so heavy it would take me ages just to put the corners in. Then I would have to vacuum the stairs, carrying this big old heavy cleaner down the stairs backwards, making sure I didn't miss any bits and praying at each step that I didn't fall.

Mother would rarely watch TV on Sundays, only the rerun of *EastEnders*. She played her stereo as she stood in the kitchen cutting the meat. I would set the table for her and make up the gravy. I'd pass her the plates as she dished up and get my siblings at the table ready to eat.

Dad would come home, half-cut, and, after we'd eaten our dinner, I'd make him a cup of tea while he play-fought with my brother. Mother would tell him what had been done that day and what still needed to be done. After Dad had his food, with half of it on the floor, he'd go to bed for a lie-down. We had to be quiet. No one was allowed upstairs and woe betide anyone who woke him. Even if Alan or Audrey disturbed him they'd get a slap and then I'd get a dig for not keeping them quiet.

Mother would never tell Dad that I was doing the ironing for her while she sat in front of the fire doing her crossword book. I was constantly running in and out of the garden telling my brother and sister to keep quiet and trying to get the ironing done.

Afterwards, I put all the clothes away and sorted the underwear into piles. Then I'd set everyone's clothes out for the following day – the school uniforms and Dad's work clothes.

When it was bath time, my brother and sister would get in first. They were still only little and loved playing with the bubbles and splashing each other. Mother would be in the kitchen making sandwiches for tea, while I washed the kids' hair and gave them the soap-lathered sponge with which to wash themselves. When Mother had finished she would call for the little ones to get out of the bath. I would wrap them in towels and take them in to her, and she would get them dried and dressed.

She would put their plates on a tray and they would go upstairs to Dad. Meanwhile, I had to get into the cold, sometimes dirty, water that my siblings had just shared. I'd wash my hair and body really quickly before jumping out. We had a heater in the bathroom which we were never allowed to use but on a Sunday, while Mother was upstairs with Dad and the kids, I'd get out of the bath and stand under it for warmth. As soon as I heard someone coming downstairs I'd switch it off, get dressed and brush my teeth.

There was only me to have my tea now, so I'd sit at the table eating my sandwiches on my own while everyone else ate cake in the lounge. After asking to be excused from the table I would run my dad's bath, make him another cup of tea and then it was bedtime. Sunday was their night out.

It was hard work but I knew if I didn't do anything wrong they couldn't beat me. I preferred this existence to the one where I was being smacked every two minutes.

On some weekends and especially during school holidays I would hang out with my cousin Paul. His mum was my mother's sister and our parents would often go out together. We would play Madonna on the stereo and dance along like we were on stage, or we would play out on our bikes. Sometimes we would play in the alley behind Paul's house with his friends. Paul was younger than me by three years, so he was still in primary school, but that didn't bother me. Paul's sister was a year older than me but we didn't have anything in common. I didn't really get on with her friends either. I was a bit jealous of her, if I'm honest. She had everything I wanted. Her home life was in no way like mine. And what I was starting to realize more and more, is that she and the other kids I saw around me were heading for a happy future, that they'd always be surrounded by their family's love, always supported. What was I heading towards, with Mother as my main example? And I couldn't do a thing about it.

Paul loved music, as did I. We would sit and write the lyrics to our favourite songs and copy dance moves from the music videos. We watched Madonna concerts over and over again and we would play the CD and pretend we were her in concert, copying her dance moves. It was so funny.

Paul wanted to be a DJ on the radio. He had all the latest records and was allowed to play his stereo whenever he wanted, whereas my parents only let me play mine on a Saturday or Sunday afternoon, but never both.

These were only brief moments of happiness however, set against a general backdrop of misery.

Paul often felt scared at my house. He was frightened of my parents. He used to say they were loud and big, and he often witnessed my beatings, which I continued to receive, often for no reason. On other occasions he saw me eating alone outside in the rain. I would ride my bike to his house and forget about home until it was time to go.

Dad used to cook pies, and we would eat them with vegetables he grew in the back garden. His rhubarb pie was horrible and bitter. We had to eat it, though, or we'd go to bed with a bloody mouth. Dad told me that the leaves on the rhubarb were poisonous.

'If you eat them you'll die,' he said.

I would watch him scrape the leaves off with a potato

peeler, then he would boil them. They smelled awful but, if I said anything, Dad saw it as a reflection on his cooking. He fancied himself as a master chef and he didn't take kindly to anyone criticizing him.

One afternoon, I was outside in the garden. My siblings were playing together on their bikes and I sat on a fern bush I had flattened. I was bored and cold and wanted to go in but was told no.

My parents were taking it in turns to watch out of the window and, if they saw me crying, I would be smacked. I sat with my head in my hands so they couldn't see my eyes. This particular afternoon, I felt so low. My whole mind was muddled with confusion.

I was a child. I didn't know what was wrong with me. All I knew was that I could see the rhubarb sticking out of the ground and I desperately wanted to eat the leaves. I tried to picture my parents saddened by my death but, deep down, I felt they wouldn't even care. I imagined my grave unkempt and overgrown. I cried even more. The pain I had in my chest felt like my heart was breaking.

The days when I felt this way became quite frequent but, even though I was a child, to me it was normal.

At school, my life was different. It was a lie, but at least it was different. Apart from Laura, no one knew the harsh realities of my home life. I was the same as everyone else, as far as they were concerned.

On Mondays the girls would talk about what they had done or where they had been. If I had been to

Laura's we'd talk about that but, if not, I'd make something up. I didn't want my friends to know I had no life. My Saturdays consisted of shopping with Mother, pushing trolleys and watching bags, or sitting in the back garden watching my siblings so Dad could watch his horse racing. Sometimes they let me listen to my stereo, but only for an hour, because it was in their room.

I couldn't dance around or have it loud because the bedroom was situated above the lounge and any banging would result in the slipper, so I would sit on the floor and sing along to the songs on the radio.

Christmas was never that exciting for me. Why would you get excited over something that just upset you? I cried every year. It was the day when it was painfully obvious I was an outsider.

Yes, they gave me some presents, normally essential clothes I needed anyway. We opened them in my parents' room. It was L-shaped and my small pile of presents was hidden in the corner under the old wooden windows, where the curtain moved because of the wind outside, mould from rainwater covered the wooden frame and the paint flicked off if you tried to wipe the sill clean.

My siblings squealed with delight as they tore into their big heaps of gifts. I wanted to be happy for them – of course I did. It wasn't their fault they were treated differently, but I couldn't help but feel sorry for myself. Sometimes I yearned for the days when I had no concept of Christmas.

I looked out of the window and saw all the other

kids with their new toy pushchairs and bikes, including my siblings, laughing with excitement, running back and forth with the different toys they had received.

The rest of Christmas Day was like any other day for me. I helped Mother with the dinner while Dad went to the pub. He'd be back in time for us all to eat together. After dinner we walked to Nan's for Christmas tea with the rest of the family.

The one exception was the year my parents gave me a bike. It was brilliant. I could actually play with the others because I had something new to show too. I loved that bike. It was blue and silver and was my freedom from the garden. On Saturdays I'd clean it diligently. I'd get a bucket of soapy water and wash it down with a sponge. Then I'd dry it off and buff it up until it gleamed.

My siblings and I rode our bikes and, when we got to Nan's, we parked them outside. We sat around waiting for everyone else to turn up and, when they did, the children had to sit and be quiet while the adults talked.

It would take one of my cousins to ask if we could go out. I wouldn't dare. My parents didn't care who was around. If they thought I was out of line they would say so.

Running out the door and jumping on to my bike was freedom. I rode up and down my nan's road twenty, maybe thirty, times, only stopping to speak to a passing cousin. Riding my bike gave me the idea that when I got older I was going to drive a car. I was going to drive so far away no one would find me.

In school I kept my family life secret from everyone. After my relationship with Abbie deteriorated I deliberately blocked anyone from becoming too close.

Occasionally, friends asked if they could stay at my house, but I lied and said either that we were going out to a family thing or there was no room. At lunchtimes I went to my nan's, because, as my parents were working, I wasn't entitled to free dinners. It was cheaper for them if I went there.

Laura went home for lunch too, so we walked together there and back. When it was home time I rode my bike back, and every time I turned the corner into my street my heart started pounding.

Every day was the same. My parents went through my stuff, searching through my room for anything incriminating. They didn't stop at room raiding. As soon as I got through the door Mother would grab my school bag and tip the contents on the floor. I don't know what she expected to find. She went through my books and read any personal notes or scraps of paper I had in there. I learned quickly not to keep a diary. She would have gone through it in an instant.

If she found anything she didn't like – no matter how inconsequential or innocent it was – I'd get a beating as soon as I got home.

The tiniest bit of paper or dirty washing on the floor would lead to a beating. I rode up the side entry to our house and parked my bike in the back garden. I knew instantly if she was in a mood by the greeting she gave me. If everything was fine I'd maybe get a 'hello'. If she met me with silence, however, I ran up the stairs, got changed and looked around to see what it was she had found.

Often I stood there scratching my head, wondering what I had done wrong. I did my homework immediately, hoping she might forget whatever it was that had put her in a mood in the first place. Sometimes it worked, and I never knew what it was that had upset her, but other times I found out only after my chores were done. Sometimes she wouldn't be in a mood at all – that was just her way of treating me. I actually think she simply didn't like talking to me. I did everything she asked of me but still she would not afford me the most basic respect.

Dad was strict with homework. He examined my homework diary every day to see what I had to do. That would have been fine – a lot of children would love for their parents to take an interest in their schoolwork – but the trouble was he barely understood the maths or English I had to do. The only time I had any interaction with my dad that didn't involve him shouting was when I asked for help. I knew what I was doing but I also worked out that if I showed him I needed his help then he would be nice to me. Often the advice he gave was wrong but I pretended I was grateful for his input.

For art, I'd say I couldn't draw certain things, so Dad would step in. His effort was invariably horrendous but I smiled and said 'thank you' and put it in my bag. I spent many a lunchtime in the school library re-doing my homework because Dad had done it wrong. Only by pretending to be stupid did I get him to talk to me like a human being.

He signed my homework diary every night and he wanted me to get my form tutor to sign it too. If she said no I panicked for the rest of the day because I knew Dad would go mad at me. Everyone else had his or her diary signed off on Monday mornings during tutorial. I couldn't tell my tutor why I needed it signed every day.

Daily life was exhausting and it felt like I was busting a gut for such scant reward that I started to bunk off school. In order to hang out with my friends I started to skip lessons. I know it was wrong, but I just wanted to rebel against something and I had no scope to step out of line at home. At first we just hung out in the toilets, ducking into a cubicle whenever the door opened in case it was a teacher. Then we started leaving the school premises, hiding by the bungalows that surrounded the school playground.

One day, a couple of friends and I decided to branch out further. One of them smoked, so we went to the shop so she could get herself a single cigarette, then we made our way to the park. We hid in the thick bushes, playing in the small stream, jumping across it, swinging on the trees and forging notes for our teachers the following day.

I also started getting to school late, only by a minute or two. I don't even know how, because I was at the school gates with the rest of the girls by 8.45 a.m. It was enough for the deputy head to phone home and report me.

She wasn't a fan of mine and she loved that my dad told her during parents' night that Mother and he would punish me if I misbehaved in her class. Any time she called, the slipper would be waiting for me when I got home.

There were times when I was actually in school, perhaps in the library re-doing homework, but if she hadn't seen me come in she assumed I was late or skiving and was straight on the phone home. I protested my innocence but it made no difference. They weren't interested.

Soon Dad started taking me to school, driving right up to the gate and escorting me in when the bell rang. My friends looked at me with sympathy on their faces, but I'd be burning red, fighting back the tears. I wanted to shout at Dad, tell him he was embarrassing me, but I didn't have the courage and so I skulked off to my registration.

His close attention didn't stop me wagging classes, though. I wish it had done, because when I got caught, it wasn't nice.

Sometimes I skipped class on my own – usually French and history – because my friends were in different lessons and wouldn't know I was bunking off. I quite liked going off on my own. I'd sit in the park thinking about anything and everything, daydreaming mainly, about what I wanted from life.

One day I was sitting there in a world of my own. BEEP!

A car pulled up next to me. It was Nan and Grand-dad. I waved, turned and started walking back towards school. I don't know why. I'd been caught.

Suddenly Mother jumped out of the back of the car. I stood frozen to the spot, waiting for the beating. Weirdly, however, she didn't go mad. She handed me the front-door key and told me to go home.

I didn't ask why. I ran, not once stopping, my throat dry from thirst, the sweat dripping down my face. As I neared the house my body started shaking with fear and excitement. I got inside and fell on to the sofa. Catching my breath, I lay there, wondering why Mother hadn't shouted.

I needed a wee. I threw my jacket on to the chair as I ran into the bathroom. After washing my hands, I came through the lounge door and looked up. Dad's car was pulling on to the drive. Panic-stricken, I started think-ing of excuses why I was home. I couldn't think of anything!

I grabbed my bag and ran upstairs. I heard the key turn in the door as I crawled under my bed.

'Collette!' he shouted.

I didn't answer. Why was he shouting for me? Surely he assumed I was at school. I could hear his footsteps coming up the stairs, slowly. I stopped breathing. I didn't want him to hear me.

There he was, standing in front of my bed. He stood

there for what seemed like an eternity. I could see his trainers. He never moved or said a word. Eventually, he started to kneel down and, lifting the quilt, stared me in the eye.

I screamed.

'Please don't hurt me,' I said, pleading. 'Mum knows.'

'Get downstairs,' he said.

I pulled myself from under the bed and followed him. As I entered the lounge, Dad looked at me.

'Get your school bag,' he said.

I did as I was told, still not knowing what he was going to do. This was worse than an actual beating. I felt like a mouse caught by a cat and being played with until it decided what to do next.

He snatched my bag out of my hand and tipped everything out on to the floor. I didn't know what he was looking for, but he flicked through every book, tipped out my pencil case, read every scrap of paper. I felt like the police had arrested me.

After he'd finished I picked everything up and put it back into the bag. Dad then picked up my coat from where I'd left it on the chair. That was how he'd known I was home. He threw it at me and walked towards the front door. I wanted to punch myself. He had only popped home to pick up his time sheets for work. If I had just grabbed my jacket he would have been in and out and I could have been sitting in front of the TV chilling out. Seeing his car had sent me into a state of panic. I hadn't thought about the jacket – just the need to hide.

In the car, not a word was said. I thought he would take me to school, but instead we went to Nan's. Mother was sitting on the sofa drinking tea when we walked in. The look on her face said 'guilty' but she denied ever giving me the key. My grandparents defended her because, when they saw me at the park, Mother told them I was going back to school. With that, Dad threw me back into the car and marched me there.

He stood in reception yelling at the secretary for allowing me to slip out. Everyone was watching. I could see people whispering and pointing. My ears were burning and I was shaking uncontrollably. The head of the school didn't punish me. My dad told him he would take care of me at home, and that was sufficient for him.

I knew what was coming. Mother blamed me for making her look bad, and she let me know it.

So much for me keeping my home life out of school. My friends never mentioned what happened but, from that day on, they got to know what my parents were really like. It was an unspoken fact that I had drawn the short straw at home.

When I was thirteen I got a paper round. It only paid £12.50 a week but that was enough for me. It meant I could have school dinners and go to after-school clubs. I played netball, but it wasn't enough. Apart from that, I was stuck in the house. Mother paid for Audrey to attend Girls' Brigade and, after I started earning money, I asked if I could go too.

'As long as you pay for it yourself,' she said.

I was ecstatic.

Girls' Brigade wasn't the first association I'd joined. For a brief spell, aged ten, I'd gone to Brownies, but Mother had refused to give me the sub money so I spent each night dodging Brown Owl when she went round collecting. It never went unnoticed, and many times they confronted Dad when he came to pick me up. He told them he'd given me the money but I must have spent it in the tuck shop. Brown Owl ran the tuck shop, so she knew this wasn't true, as I never had money for sweets. My parents stopped picking me up after that, and soon I stopped going, because I ran out of excuses why I didn't have the money. At least with the Girls' Brigade I wouldn't have those problems.

I loved it instantly. I played the drums and paid for my uniform weekly. The organizers didn't know it was my money. They thought my mother was wonderful because she would help them with the younger ones. My sister was an Explorer, so she went at a different time to me. Our practice sessions were later in the evening. I paid for my own drumsticks and tapped away for hours, practising whenever I could.

The best time, however, was when we went camping. Again, I paid for it myself, but it was worth it. I had the time of my life. I wasn't scared of the dark or the bugs. Lying in my tent, I felt a million miles from home – a feeling I still get when I accomplish something. It was pure contentment and happiness.

Eating cold baked beans and marshmallows was the

life I wanted. There was no one to tell me to go to sleep. I could have midnight feasts, this time consisting of crisps and chocolate, not tissue paper.

The night before we were due to go home I sneaked out of my tent and walked around the woods, stepping on twigs and cones in my bare feet. It felt so good. I found a log to sit on and watched the moon and stars moving across the sky.

I so didn't want to go home.

I'd just had five days of activities and fun, with adults who weren't strict and who spoke to us like they would to other human beings. We weren't forced into chores, but if we did them they rewarded us. In the mornings we would clear breakfast things away, tidy our tents and then spend the rest of the day playing on the obstacle course.

On the coach trip home I must have been noticeably quiet, because everyone kept asking if I was OK. I nodded but, inside, I was anything but OK. I was dreading going home, back to Mother and the bleakness of my blighted life.

IO

When I returned home from camp I fell right back into my place – cleaning, cooking and looking after my siblings.

Mother started working in the evenings as a cleaner so it was my job to look after Alan and Audrey until Dad got back. Mother left at 4 p.m. and Dad would be home for five. During this hour I had to finish off dinner, dish up, wash up and have the kids bathed. When Dad came home I would fetch his dinner, make him a drink, then it was homework time. Dad picked Mother up at six thirty, taking the younger kids with him, while I finished my homework and cleaned up for Mother coming home.

One evening I was sorting out the dinner when there was a knock on the door. It was Phil. He was looking for Mother and me. Before we'd left the Greenford estate, Phil used to visit when Dad was at work. He would tell me he was my dad, not Dave. He would shower me with attention and we would have fun. I didn't tell him any of my secrets, though, because he was a crazy man and it scared me. I suspected he would kill for me, but I couldn't tell him things because I felt he was always in and out of my life.

When we left that flat, however, Mother didn't tell Phil where we were going. I thought he'd forgotten about me. Dave had said he was my dad and that Phil was nothing to me.

Seeing him standing there in his leathers, I suddenly started to panic.

'Don't worry,' he said. 'I'll be gone soon.'

I called him in and made him a coffee while I sorted out the kids. They were at the table eating their tea, and I sat in the window talking to Phil, keeping a look-out for Dad. Phil told me how angry he was with Mother for taking me away. He said no matter where we went he would always be my dad and he'd always love me.

He held out his hand and gave me a pound. He then cupped my face with his hands and planted a kiss on me. It sounds stupid, but I actually felt like his daughter, so much so that when he left and my brother asked who he was I said: 'He is MY dad.'

Within ten minutes of Phil leaving, Dad pulled up. The relief that came over me almost made me cry. I had so many different emotions I felt it was too much to deal with.

I hurried into the kitchen and flicked on the kettle. My brother and sister ran into the lounge, arms outstretched for their dad. They were always excited to see him. I was in my own little bubble. I kept replaying the conversation with Phil in my head. He said he was my dad and that he loved me. That was all I needed, the knowledge that someone was actually thinking about me and genuinely loved me.

I set Dad's dinner down on the coffee table and was washing up when he called me into the lounge. My brother was standing there staring at me, twisting the bottom of his jumper between his fingers. My sister was sitting on Dad's lap with her arms wrapped around him. She wouldn't look at me. No one had to say anything. I knew he knew. There was no point in denying it.

Dad said he'd seen Phil's bike parked outside and had waited to see if he came out of the house. Of course he did. And I'd stood there and waved him off, praying I'd see him again soon and that he would take me away from my parents.

Dave went mental. He took the kids to get Mother, but within ten minutes he was back. He left the kids in the car as he came charging into my room. He shouted that Phil had kidnapped Mother and that he was going to look for her.

'God help you when we get back,' he said. 'This is all your fault.'

Then he left, slamming the front door behind him. In a heartbeat I jumped out of bed, threw on my clothes and grabbed my school bag. I tipped everything on to my bed and stuffed the bag with pyjamas and clothes. I ran out of the back door, threw my bag over my bike handles and pedalled. In my mind I knew straight away where I was going, but I kept thinking about the reaction I was going to get back home.

If Dad couldn't find Mother, he was going to kill me. That's what he'd said, and I had no reason to doubt him.

It took me for ever to travel the four miles to the Greenford estate, but I was quietly surprised that I managed not to get lost. I knocked on Stephanie's door. It was weird being back again, but the fear of seeing my parents outweighed any other.

I sat and cried my heart out to Sue. She comforted me and held me until the sobs subsided. She sent Stephanie and me outside to play. I honestly thought I was going to live there. I pictured myself being part of the family, being Stephanie's sister and having the freedom to be a child. I crossed over the road and played with other kids in the street. I was never allowed to before but, in my head, I no longer had parents so I could do whatever I wanted. I even went to the park, but I got scared because the slide was too high.

On the way back to Stephanie's flat I spotted something familiar. It was Dad's car.

'I'm not going back!' I screamed.

Stephanie said her mum wouldn't let me go back, I could stay with her for ever, so I walked back confidently. As we walked through the door I saw Mother. She was safe, but we walked in as she was telling Sue about Phil.

'She told him where I was,' she said, pointing at me. She went on that Phil had forced her to go with him.

'I never told him anything,' I tried to interrupt. He

had never asked where Mother was. He had only wanted to know about me, but no one would listen.

I had no say in anything. Sue said she'd had to phone Nan to get my parents' number. They needed to know where I was. Before they took me home, Sue spoke to me. 'If you're good, you can stop at weekends,' she said.

I looked at Stephanie. We both knew this was never going to happen.

When we got home nothing was said. They sent me to bed, and that was it. No one talked to me, not even my sister. We still shared a room, but when I called her name she turned her back to me. When I persisted she shouted, 'Dad!' Both Mother and Dad came up and cuddled her, telling her to ignore me. They then kissed her and left.

I don't even know why, but I cried. It was an every-day occurrence – her being showered with love in front of me – but that night it got to me so much. Things were the same as they'd always been, I suppose, but it was hitting me harder and harder. How were things ever going to get any better?

That summer we went on holiday to Paignton in Devon. We went there most years, staying in a caravan in the same holiday resort. On each visit we 'ooh'ed and 'aah'ed at all the new gadgets it had, as each year we upgraded to a better one than before.

Holidays were the only time, apart from Christmas,

that I got new clothes. Mother never let me choose and they were never makes or brands you had heard of, but I didn't mind. At least they were new. She never allowed any of us to wear them before we went and the week before our departure Dad would go mad about the washing, and about how much Mother would have to do when we got back. As a result, we had to wear the same jeans and top for the week, with the only clean items being our underwear.

The first day of the holiday was a godsend, not least because it meant we could wear new, clean clothes. The night before we left we had to be in bed by 6 p.m. Dad would then have us up at 4 a.m. to be on the road by five.

We'd fall asleep in the car, listening to Mother's tapes. She loved Cliff Richard, folk and country and western music. She'd blast Foster and Allen like everyone wanted to hear. Embarrassed wasn't the word for how I'd feel. Sometimes, though, I'd sing along because boredom would set in and the only way to pass the time was to sing.

Once, I sang the wrong words for Cliff's 'Bachelor Boy'. Mother's head swivelled like something from *The Exorcist*, her green eyes glowing like they had light bulbs behind them. I was staring that hard at her I didn't see her left hand swing round the back of her seat and catch me in the face.

'You stupid black bitch. You don't even know the fucking words,' she said. Then she turned round and carried on singing. I never sang after that.

When we got to the holiday park, we were early, as usual. We always got there for 10 a.m., but we couldn't get into the caravan until two in the afternoon. Dad took us to the clubhouse and, while he and Mother sank beer after beer, I sat nursing a glass of Coke, looking out of the window and watching all the other kids jumping in the pool, playing, splashing, giggling, having fun with their parents.

I so wanted to go in the pool. It was late August and the sun was blazing. I was in jeans and a T-shirt – our travelling clothes – and the sweat was dripping down the side of my face.

Mother didn't let us go in the pool.

'We've got a whole week here,' she said. 'Don't be ungrateful.'

At two o'clock we picked up our keys and set off to our caravan, but first we had to find the shop and stock up on teabags and milk. In the caravan, I put the kettle on and sat around while my parents decided who would have which room. My parents took the double, naturally; my sister and I got the twin room, with two tiny beds and only enough room for one person to stand in there at a time; and my brother would get the pull-out double bed in the lounge/dining area. This was our home for the week.

Every day we went to the café for breakfast, down to the beach for the day, then to the café for tea and back to the caravan for a shower to get ready for the club at night. My parents liked to sit in the same seats night after night. If they were running late getting ready, they sent me over to save the table for when they got there.

The night always started with party dances, and every night I had to get up and dance with my siblings. If I didn't my parents would shout and swear about how ungrateful I was and how I spoiled everything. People stared at us; other kids stood away from me because of my parents' language.

If a girl did speak to me, invariably they'd ask why my parents were calling me names. They always thought they mustn't be my real mum and dad because of the way they spoke to me. When I said they were the look on their faces was always pure shock. I think it's safe to say I didn't really make many friends on holiday.

My parents took bingo extremely seriously. I sat and watched as they frantically marked off the numbers, hoping to win the house money. If they didn't, they'd complain it was a fix. They forbade me from going to the toilet while the bingo was on, so I made sure I went while they sold the books, even if I didn't need to, forcing myself so I wouldn't need to go while they were playing.

One night I held it in and got such bad pain in my kidney I couldn't move. I didn't tell my parents; they were engrossed in the bingo and we weren't allowed to talk. I had on a long denim skirt and a white top and I started rocking back and forth. Dad smacked my leg and told me to sit still. I tried, but my legs started shaking. Someone shouted, 'House!' and I jumped up and ran as fast as I could to the toilet, but it was too late. Just as I closed the cubicle door the warmth started dripping down my leg. Before I could stop and think I quickly tore off my pants and threw them in the bin. My knee-high socks were wet around the top, so I rolled them down. I listened as the host repeated the numbers over the microphone, and washed my hands, drying them on my skirt, before running back to my seat just as the caller started on the next set of numbers. My parents shot me a dirty look, but keeping the kids quiet made them happy enough.

When the cabaret came on – a singer or dancer – and Mother wanted to dance I had to go with her. If she wanted to go to the toilet Dad sent me with her to make sure she was OK.

I always used to wonder whether it shouldn't be the other way around.

If I needed the toilet, I had to go on my own. No one checked whether I was OK, even though I panicked if there was a queue – not because my parents worried, but because they would go mad if I was a long time.

I also had to keep my brother and sister occupied, keeping them off the dance floor while the show was on. My parents wanted to enjoy their night; they didn't want to be getting up and down all the time. That was my job.

It was on this holiday that my parents met a family from London. Clark and Cheryl were a couple with three children – two boys and a girl. Cheryl's brother was with them too.

They looked like bikers, with their leather jackets, ripped jeans and long, greasy hair. Their children were cute; they were only small, with the youngest about two years old. At the time, they were just people my parents were speaking to. When the holiday ended, they vowed to keep in touch. I doubted I would ever see them again, though. Little did I know that I *was* going to see them again, and very soon, and that they would be part of yet another troubling episode in my life.

11

A few months after we returned from Devon my parents announced they were getting married. It wasn't open for discussion. They'd be doing it in April the following year. I wasn't sure how I felt about that. Strangely detached, I suppose is how I'd put it. It really made no difference to me.

My parents had kept in touch with Clark and Cheryl, the biker family from London, and, as if they were long-lost friends, invited them to stay with us two days before the ceremony.

That night, the adults all went to the pub, leaving me, a thirteen-year-old, to look after five kids all under the age of seven. I was in bed by the time they came home, sleeping – until the loud music and laughter started.

The following day Cheryl went to hospital with pneumonia. Mother was upset, because it meant she wouldn't be at the wedding. She sent me to Nan's that afternoon as the hairdresser was coming for my cousins, my sister and me, because we were all bridesmaids. Wendy was Mother's matron of honour. She was also in hospital at the time, because she had problems with her kidneys, but she was allowed out to attend the wedding, as long as she returned the following day.

Mother wanted our hair curly. Mine already was, but I still had to have the curlers in. My sister was the only one who didn't have to have it done because she was too young and her hair too short and fine.

That evening, Mother had her hen party and Dad his stag do. Again, they left me to look after the kids. Dad came home drunk and I had to help him up the stairs and on to the bed. I took off his jacket, shoes and socks, covered him over and went to bed.

The wedding was the next day and I had to have a bath and bathe Alan and Audrey before I could think about leaving the house. I had to catch the bus with my sister, with rollers in my hair. I walked to the bus stop, passing people I knew, hanging my head and pretending not to see them. On the bus, I stared out of the window, trying not to catch people's eye.

When we got off the bus, we walked up the long, steep road to my nan's. Friends from school lived on that road. I dragged my sister up that hill as quickly as I could. I didn't want people to see me with huge rollers in my hair.

After all that, the wedding was lovely. Mother wore her sister's wedding dress and she arrived at the church before my dad. For a moment I wondered if he was going to turn up. When he did, I was gutted.

The party threatened to boil over on a couple of occasions, but that was the norm for any party featuring my mother.

That night, she went to the hospital, still in her dress,

to see Cheryl. It was a rare moment of compassion from her.

Cheryl left hospital a couple of days later and, as she and Clark got ready to go back to London, things got really weird. On the day they went home, as Cheryl and Clark loaded their car with their things, Mother put a case in the boot of Dad's car. I don't know where my siblings were. I just remember getting in the car, Dad in the driver's seat, and following Clark and Cheryl out of the city. After a while I plucked up the courage to ask where we were going.

'London,' Mother said. That was it.

My parents spoke between themselves the whole journey. I coughed now and then to let them know I was still there, only to be shot a look from Dad in the rear-view mirror. We arrived in London and pulled up on an estate, parking outside a block of flats. We followed Cheryl and Clark and their children inside and used the lift to take us up to the top floor.

There was such a strong stench of urine that I had to cover my mouth with my coat sleeve. Dad pulled my arm down. In the flat it didn't smell much better. There was rubbish strewn everywhere, empty beer cans lay crushed on the floor, the sink was piled high with washing-up. To sit down we had to move the washing that was stacked up hiding the sofa. This was clearly their flat.

I knelt on the floor and played with their little girl, helping her put shapes into a ball. Every time she put a shape into the right hole a tune played and she squealed with excitement. After about an hour my parents stood up. I followed and we got to the front door. My parents each kissed my head, then left. I stood there motionless. Where had they gone? Had they given me away? Didn't they want me any more? I looked around and Clark was bringing the suitcase up the stairs.

Cheryl called me through and showed me where I would be sleeping and where I could put my case. I opened it and found my clothes in it. I was sharing a room with the little girl. My bed was a sleeping bag on the floor and there was no room to hang my stuff anywhere. I would be living out of my suitcase.

Over the next few days I didn't hear from my parents and the couple I was staying with never mentioned them either. It was horrible. I didn't know what to make of it. I wasn't being beaten but, if anything, this was mental torture. I had no idea what was happening or how long this situation would go on for.

Nobody would tell me anything.

Clark and Cheryl loved their beer, and they didn't sleep much. The whole family was up for six in the morning. No one told me. I was ready for breakfast by seven thirty, but I was too late, apparently, so I didn't eat until teatime. They didn't eat lunch. They were too twisted to move.

I spent the day playing with the children and cleaning. We didn't leave the flat. Clark went to the shops, but neither of them worked. They were too lazy. When teatime came round, I was starving. When Cheryl served dinner she put a huge dollop of ketchup on it. I liked tomato sauce, but not with everything. I was to discover they liked ketchup with anything – even as a substitute for gravy on roast dinners.

The next day was the same as the day before. We didn't leave the flat but Clark went out to the shops to get food for tea. I tried to tell them I didn't like ketchup, but my dinner was served swimming in the stuff.

'Eat it or leave it,' they said. I left it.

For two weeks I lived like this, out of my suitcase, playing with the little girl, hardly having anything to eat, wondering if this was my life now.

Then, without warning, my parents turned up on the doorstep. I had never been so happy to see them. On the way home I told them about the food and how I wouldn't eat.

'You shouldn't have been so fussy,' Mother said. 'If you went hungry it was your own fault.'

I never found out why they sent me there. Perhaps they wanted some alone time, as they didn't have a proper honeymoon. However, my brother and sister stayed with them at the house. Maybe they just wanted family time.

I *was* the odd one out, after all.

Even though I was earning my own money, it was never enough. I was never allowed pocket money, yet I was also expected to use my money to buy things for my brother and sister. If I was getting sweets or ice cream

I had to buy them something too. If I ran out of money, I racked up a bill with Dad. He'd buy the ice creams and ice pops, but I had to pay him back.

It got to the point when I was too scared to ask for any more. So when I started my lady month and I ran out of money to buy proper sanitary towels, I used folded-up tissue paper instead. Every morning I got up at 6 a.m., got ready for school and headed off for my paper round. I did it again after school and at weekends.

Every week, my money went straight into Dad's hands. Even after I paid back the money I owed, my parents viewed it as my 'rent'. When I turned fourteen, I gave up the paper round.

Our neighbours, the Bakers, were going through a rough patch in their marriage so Jack, who was a year older than me, started sneaking round to our house when his parents went out. One day, they went shopping and came back earlier than he thought. Jack ran out of the back door and climbed the fence to his garden. There was a shed on the other side and he climbed from the fence on to the roof, but as he jumped he dropped his trainer and had to climb back up to get it. I laughed so much – it was the funniest thing I'd ever seen.

Eventually, however, Jack's parents split up and he stayed at the family home with his dad, brother and sister. He spent most of his time round our house, though. We became really good friends, sitting in the back garden, talking about our families. I didn't need to tell him much because he heard it all through the bedroom walls. His parents were completely different. They loved him and cared about him and wanted the best for him. The split tore him apart.

Every Tuesday night Dad went to the pub to play snooker, and sometimes Jack's dad would go with him. My mother loved jigsaws so every Tuesday night Jack and I would sit on the floor with her trying to do a 5,000-piece puzzle. Soon we would get bored and start messing about, chucking cushions and pretend fighting. I don't know why we did it, because we knew it annoyed Mother and she would always send me to bed.

One evening, we were mucking about as usual and Mother shouted at me to get to bed. Jack tried to defend me, saying we were only playing, and we'd stop, but she was having none of it. It was as if pure evil took hold of her.

One minute I was rolling on the floor giggling and the next I saw Mother come running out the kitchen with the mop. She shoved the mop head right in my face.

'Get your arse to bed,' she said.

I shot up and ran, but Mother followed me, catching my ankles with the mop handle. I could hear Jack shouting at her to stop. I ran into the bedroom but, instead of diving under the cover and hiding, I crouched in the corner.

I started screaming and shouting: 'I hate my life! I hate my family!'

My arms covered my head. There was so much

banging and shouting I didn't have a clue what was going on or who was where. I could still hear Jack yelling at Mother to calm down, but it wasn't close; they were downstairs.

I started to stand up, but then I heard footsteps. I ducked back down. Suddenly Mother was standing on my bed looking down at me. I looked up and caught a glint of metal. She was holding a big kitchen carving knife above her head, ready to plunge it down at me.

Everything seemed to freeze. In that split instant I prepared myself to die. I could picture what heaven was like – a place of love and peace where I would finally be free.

Jack dived on top of Mother. They both fell on to the bed. I jumped up and ran down the stairs. Mother came after me, with Jack behind her. She was about to grab me when Jack pushed her into the kitchen. I ran back up the stairs and jumped into bed, waiting.

It seemed like ages, but eventually I slowly pulled the quilt away from my head. I couldn't hear anything. I went to the top of the stairs and listened. The TV was blaring and now I could hear Mother tinkering about in the kitchen. I pulled on my slippers and dressing gown over the top of my nightdress. I crept down the stairs and opened the front door, very quietly and gently, hands shaking, not really having a plan.

As soon as the front door opened, I held my breath and ran. I had to get away. My own mother wanted to kill me. That wasn't normal. I could still see the crazed look in her eyes, her pure conviction in what she was about to do.

It was dark and quiet. The only sound was from the passing traffic. I ran up to the main road. People in cars were looking at me. I was running in the streets in my nightwear, but I didn't care. With tears streaming down my face, I carried on running, ducking into people's gardens whenever I saw anyone out walking.

The main road I was on had houses on one side and a graveyard on the other. It was quite poorly lit, so hiding was easy, behind hedges and cars. I made it all the way to the pub where Dad was – but what was I going to do now?

I sat in the bushes underneath the motorway bridge, freezing and scared. I sat and watched as taxis pulled in and out of the car park to the pub. People were laughing and having a good time. I started to panic. I hadn't thought this through properly.

If I went into the pub, Dad would be angry because I'd be disturbing him on his night out. If I went home, Mother would be waiting for me. I didn't know what to do.

I walked back home, taking my time, thinking that the longer I took the more worried Mother would be and Dad would be home sooner. I turned the corner on to our street. The front door was closed. Mother must know I'd sneaked out. Should I knock on the door? No way!

I crept up the entry and into the back garden. I ran

to the bottom of the garden and hid behind the apple tree. I couldn't hide behind the hedge where the shed was because it was too dark and scary. I just sat and watched the house, wondering what was going on inside. Was Mother worried? Was Jack still there? I waited and waited. Then the back door opened, the kitchen light flooded the garden and, as my eyes adjusted, I saw a figure in the doorway. A hand touched my shoulder and I jumped. My heart was in my throat. I spun round, and there stood Jack. He helped me up and tried to coax me back towards the house.

I started screaming and digging my heels into the ground, but my slippers had no grip. Then I heard another voice. Not Mother or Dad. It was Jack's dad.

'Come to ours, babe, it's over now.'

I followed Jack and his dad down the garden through the entry and round the front to their house. Once in there, I started to relax. It felt so warm and calm. Jack wrapped a blanket round my shoulders while his sister made me a cup of tea. It was half filled with sugar but I was told to drink it, as it would help with the shock.

As I was explaining to Jack where I had gone, my dad walked in. The room went silent. I couldn't look at him. I was waiting for him to start shouting and blaming me. Instead, he grabbed me and held me so tight, constantly saying sorry, over and over again. I was numb. It must have been the first time he had shown affection towards me. I was confused.

I stayed the night at Jack's, and the following morning Dad took Mother to the doctor. Apparently she was unwell, and she was put on to some sort of mood stabilizer.

Again, she acted as if nothing had happened. Like every flashpoint, it was never discussed again – like it was normal for a mother to go for her child with a knife. I dared not say anything. Was I ever going to break free of her?

The medication calmed Mother down for a while and slowly we got back to our old routine. Dad went back to his nights out and Mother allowed me to stay up that bit longer. When they went out together, my parents gave me the responsibility of babysitting.

Jack sat with me and we'd watch *Carry On* films or *On the Buses*. The only stipulation was that I had to be in bed when they got home. Jack and I often lay opposite each other on the sofa and play fought by kicking each other or having pillow fights. We grew so close that I started hanging out with him and his brother, Mike. We could only play out the front of the house, because I still wasn't allowed to go anywhere else, but it was fun. We would chase each other back and forth over the road and play Kerby. The older lads would drink cans of lager while Jack ran up and down the street with me on his back. Even though we were messing about, I started to feel more grown up.

On Sundays we walked the nearly three miles to Wyndley baths. For a short cut we climbed over the fence into the golf course and ran across the fairway, invariably getting caught and shouted at. We were doing no harm, but I didn't tell my parents about being caught or they would've stopped me going. It was freedom from the house, and the less they knew the better. Swimming was free at the baths, so my parents were OK with me going but, after I had enjoyed only a few weeks of freedom, they demanded I start taking my brother. All the lads would be splashing about in the deep end, diving off the boards and dunking each other, while I had to stay with my brother in the shallow end, too low to even have a swim. Babysitting my brother defeated the purpose of going, so I stopped. There was no point. I might as well stay in.

Mother's medicine seemed to calm her down slightly, but make no mistake: she would still fly off the handle at the slightest thing. The tablets weren't a miracle cure by any means.

She said she was ill but, if I mentioned the pills, she would tell Dad that I was making fun of her, and, instead of her punishing me, he would do it.

We had never been close, but Mother and I were growing further and further apart. I was fourteen and I had no love for her at all, and none for Dad. I was counting down the years until I was able to leave home. I survived by agreeing to everything they said, doing whatever they wanted me to do, handing over whatever money I made. It was all about existing.

For a short period I did start answering back, but

only when there were other people around. My parents had at least learned not to beat me in front of people. Dad was happy knowing now that all the blame was placed on Mother and her illness. He had got away with it – or so he thought.

I was sitting in the lounge reading my book one day when Dad started barking his orders: he wanted a cup of tea, his slippers fetched and the potatoes peeled. Mother sat in front of the fire, smoking like a chimney.

I was lost in the fairy tale, pretending I was the princess in the book. Dad made me jump with his deep, menacing voice. I rolled my eyes and placed my book on the chair. As I stepped into the kitchen, Dad yelled: 'Get your arse in here and stand up straight when I'm talking to you.'

'Don't you roll your eyes at me,' he said. 'While you're living under our roof, you do as you're bloody told.'

'Yes, Dad,' I said, and turned back into the kitchen.

I didn't get upset this time. I gave myself praise for being brave, and thought about being a parent myself. My children were never going to be slaves; they were going to be happy and loved.

As I carried on daydreaming, I didn't notice that Mother had gone upstairs until she came back down and demanded a black bin bag. I took Dad his cup of tea and handed Mother the bag. She called me to follow her up the stairs. I was clueless as to what was going on. I made a quick checklist in my head: the bed was made, the dirty clothes were in the wash basket, there were no shoes on the floor, all my schoolwork was completed and in my school bag. I reached my bedroom door and heard Mother shaking open the black bag. Then I heard ripping. She was tearing off all my posters from the bedroom wall. The only ones she left were my sister's. It had taken me ages to collect those posters. I'd ripped them out of magazines, or friends had passed on the ones they didn't want – posters of Bros, Kriss Kross, MC Hammer.

'What are you doing?' I said. 'Why are you doing this?'

Mother didn't answer. She had a look of crazed satisfaction on her face. I grabbed Dad's slippers from their bedroom and ran downstairs. I told him what Mother was doing and he just sat there and said he knew.

'Why?' I said, still completely baffled.

'Since you packed up your paper round and aren't bringing any money into the house, you're not allowed posters or to listen to your music again.'

I couldn't believe it. It must have slipped their minds that I already did more than my fair share of chores and that I babysat three or four times a week, even though I was still only fourteen.

I could feel something building inside me. I tried not to say it, but I couldn't help myself. The anger was growing. I pinched myself to stop exploding and covered my mouth, but the words still came out.

'I hate you!' I yelled. 'You're not my dad. I want to leave home!'

He just looked at me. He didn't care. It was all about them and what they could take from me. Nothing more.

After Mother cleared out my room and went downstairs I sat on the bed. I continued pinching myself, trying to focus my mind. The pain from squeezing my skin overrode my anger.

In the days and weeks that followed I used this tactic when Mother beat me. It seemed to work, even though she was using me like a punchbag. I didn't get away with it for long, though. She soon clued on to what I was doing and, one time, when I didn't show any emotion after one of her slaps, she grabbed a chunk of skin on my arm between her fingers and twisted.

I watched her face as she did it. It was all screwed up and contorted in hate. She bit down on her bottom lip as she applied even more pressure. She started smiling – actually smiling – as she twisted harder and harder until, finally, I couldn't resist any longer and the tears ran down my cheeks. The violent red mark stung for a day afterwards and bruised the deepest black.

I needed to find another outlet for my anger and frustration, not just from the beatings I endured but also from the verbal abuse.

If she wasn't laying into me with her hands, she was calling me all sorts of names. Bitch. Slag. Nigger. Paki. Lesbian. Tramp. Ugly.

I was all of those things to her. At other times I was a 'waste of space' and 'I shouldn't have been born', or 'I should've stayed in care.'

Listening to the barrage of abuse every day wore me down. Silence became my friend. Family was my enemy.

One day I found a paper clip and started to play Noughts and Crosses on the dry skin on my thighs. It stung at first, but then it felt comforting. I straightened the clip out and used the pointed end to draw and write on my body.

With each passing day I dug deeper and deeper until I bled. I always made sure I had jeans or trousers to cover up the scars. If I couldn't find a paper clip I'd use something else, sometimes a coarse brush, and I scratched my legs until the skin was red raw.

The scabs were red and unsightly, but it was a small cross to bear for the pure relief it gave me.

In the wake of Mother's tantrums, which showed no signs of abating, Dad said I could stay with my aunt Wendy for a while. I couldn't believe it. For the first time in my fourteen years I was getting some time away from these tyrants.

Finally, I thought, I had a passport out of this misery. I couldn't have been more wrong.

12

Out of all my family, Wendy was the one I was closest to. She didn't agree with the way my parents treated me and, because she was tired of arguing with Mother all the time, she stayed away.

When Wendy was young she was playing Snakes and Ladders next to the gas fire when her nightdress caught alight. The accident caused burns all over her body and infections that damaged her kidneys, stunting her growth. Her skin was left so tight she had to have numerous grafts and, as a result, could not have children of her own.

Wendy went for dialysis three times a week and during school holidays my parents let me go with her. I got to know all the doctors and nurses on the unit and was soon able to hook Wendy up to the machine and get it going for her. She spent four hours each time on it.

Before going to the hospital we would go into town and stop off at the newsagent's and buy lots of 'goodies'. We'd have cans of pop, sweets, chocolate, crisps and magazines and, when we got to the unit, we'd share them out with the other patients. We often got told off for giving the patients sweets, as some of them were on strict diets, but Wendy would just laugh and hand them out anyway.

I became so inspired by Wendy and her treatment that I asked to do some work experience in the dialysis unit of the children's hospital. The nurses didn't allow me to touch the machines, but I sat and spoke to the kids and their families. I drew pictures with them and read stories. I also helped out on reception, booking in appointments, finding files and taking them to the right departments. I felt really grown up.

Sadly, they only let me stay for a week, so I did a second placement in a school. I enjoyed it, but not as much as the hospital. I decided, though, that I wanted to help children in some capacity; not to be a nurse, but to look after them in some way.

Wendy was in a relationship with a man named Tom, but she wasn't happy with him at all. She might not have been able to have children, but that didn't stop her living life to the full. She enjoyed going out and spending money on new clothes. When I went to live with her I had the best clothes money could buy.

Friends at school commented on how much I had changed and I credited Wendy for everything. For the first time in my life I actually looked forward to going home and helping with dinner. Then, often we'd go and visit Wendy's friends.

Wendy also liked to go to the bingo. She knew almost everyone there. I remember going as a child when the whole family went and Nan would bring cheese and ham cobs and crisps. We hadn't been for ages, so when I went with Wendy it was weird having people saying hello and asking how my parents were.

I didn't have to go with Wendy but I was enjoying my freedom and liked taking in everything going on around me.

It was at a youth club that I met my first boyfriend. His name was Lee and, like me, he was mixed race. I got butterflies in my stomach every time I saw him. He was older than me and had his own flat. I was shocked when he told Wendy he was interested in me. No one had 'fancied' me before. He was eighteen, so I lied and said I was fifteen, almost sixteen, when really I was fourteen, nearly fifteen. If he knew the truth I didn't think he would stick around.

Some nights I sat with Wendy in the club and Lee tapped the window and gestured for me to go outside. He wasn't allowed to enter the club because he had been banned. I know it sounds bad, and I hope I know better now, but it was so exciting going out with a boy who didn't care about rules. He drank and took drugs, and sometimes would turn up late to see me because he had 'work' to do.

Even though Lee was older than me, he never once tried to push me into anything. I asked if I could try his spliff once, and he grabbed me in a headlock. He was only playing about, but then he got serious.

'Don't go down the same path as me,' he said.

When he told me I was beautiful and that I wasn't to

get held back by people like him, I shrugged it off. I was fourteen and infatuated with him. Outside, we would stand and hold each other and talk about our childhoods.

The only thing I told him was the reason I was living with Wendy: I didn't get on with my parents. He tried to question me but, when he saw I was getting uncomfortable, he left it.

One night, I didn't go to the club and Wendy told him everything about me. The next time I saw him he was angry. Not with me – he wanted revenge on my parents. This was what I had feared. I didn't feel I had any choice but to end the relationship. I was too scared of what might happen. I knew my parents, but I also knew Lee's background. It was a risk I wasn't old enough to take.

Another night, Wendy and I were in the club, and I was sitting, ripping apart beer mats, when I saw Dad.

'Collette!' he shouted from across the room.

I sat up and smiled, but Wendy jumped up immediately, ran over to him and started edging him towards the exit. As quick as he was there, he was gone again.

I ran outside. Wendy was speaking to my dad by the car. I hid around the corner so he wouldn't see me. Then I saw Lee, standing on top of a dirt-patch hill, watching her. I called him, and he walked over to me slowly, never once taking his eyes off Wendy. Then the car door closed and Dad drove off.

Wendy came over to us. She was shaking. Dad had

gone mad that I was out on a school night. 'He says you've to go home tomorrow,' she said, her face white.

I fell to my knees. It was like someone had passed sentence on me. I started crying. I was going to get a beating for this. I should have known that one day I would have to go back.

Lee freaked out. He was angry on my behalf. He started smashing the windows of the club with his fists. We tried to stop him, but he ran away. The manager came out but we said it was kids who had run off.

Wendy and I walked to the bus stop in complete silence. I could tell she was scared too.

'I'm sorry,' I said, but she just shook her head.

It was all my fault.

Waiting for the bus seemed to take for ever. It was freezing and late. I needed my bed. I needed the strength to go back home and face my demons – my parents.

From nowhere, Lee suddenly appeared.

'Just stay,' he said. 'Don't go back.'

Wendy laughed at him but I was seriously thinking about it.

'Come and live with me,' he said, 'in my flat. I'll look after you. Your parents can't get you there.'

I so wanted to believe that, but I couldn't. It was impossible. I was only fifteen. I had to go home. I kissed Lee one last time and got on the bus.

If it wasn't for Wendy I believe I wouldn't have got on the bus that night. I wanted to disappear and Lee was my only way of doing that. But I let him go.

I watched as he slowly faded away into the darkness, taking with him, it seemed, my only chance of starting life again.

The following day I went to school as usual but, instead of catching the number 65 bus back to Wendy's, I came out to find Dad waiting for me in the car outside the school gates.

He had already been to Wendy's to collect my stuff and when I got home I found my clothes strewn across my bed. I started hanging up my things and made up my bed. Mother had stripped it when I left and had never made it up again. My sister's toys were all over the floor so I picked them up and put them away in their rightful places. Then I went downstairs and sat on the chair waiting for a list of chores or a telling-off. But my parents didn't pay any attention to me. They had come into some money and so were too busy rubbing their hands together planning their night out.

Not long after I returned home I started to feel pain in my left side and I needed to go to the toilet a lot. Dad booked me an appointment with the doctor and he came in with me for my consultation. The doctor said I had a kidney infection and prescribed an antibiotic that I had to take three times a day. The pain got worse, to the point where I couldn't stand and walk. Moving just an inch produced a stabbing pain, like a hot poker in my side.

Dad took me to the children's hospital, where a doctor and nurses poked and prodded and questioned me.

On one occasion a nurse asked Dad to leave the cubicle while she examined me. When he left she held my hand and looked at me with sympathy in her eyes.

'Are you being abused?' she said.

I was stunned. I had a kidney infection, and she was asking me about abuse.

If I told her about the beatings, my parents would kill me! I thought about the time I told my school about the violence. I felt they had believed them over me. If she thought I was going to tell her what was happening at home, then she thought wrong, I wasn't about to make the same mistake twice.

'No,' I said quietly.

She allowed Dad back in.

Over the next three months I went back and forth to the hospital with infection after infection. I lost a lot of time at school but Dad went in every other day to collect homework for me. It didn't matter how much pain I was in, I had to do it. Sometimes, however, it was nice to have something with which to pass the time.

I wasn't allowed to leave my bed. I was locked away in my room all day. I stared out of my window and watched the birds in the sky, wondering where they were heading. As soon as I heard the lounge door open I climbed back into bed and pretended to be asleep. Even though I was in quite a lot of pain, I was beaten if they caught me out of bed.

The pain from the infections was like a burning sensation. Sometimes it got so much I started to feel numb and light-headed. I don't know if I passed out through the pain or fell asleep crying.

When eventually I was strong enough, Mother got me a job at Kwik Save on the high street. My shifts were Thursdays and Fridays from four until eight and all day Saturday. I worked on the tills and stacked the shelves. As I was only fifteen, I couldn't serve alcohol or tobacco. I had to ask a colleague to watch me if I had to serve a customer any of those. I made plenty of friends working there and had fun with the customers too.

I loved my job. It gave me back some of my independence. I earned £52 a week, which was a lot of money for me, but I spent it wisely. Mainly it went on school dinners and toiletries, because my parents wouldn't pay for the things I needed. They said it wasn't their responsibility.

I got paid on Fridays and, after my shift, Dad would be waiting to pick me up. I had to buy him a packet of cigarettes to say thank you. Once the shift ended it was always a rush to get my things and get out, because if I kept him waiting for more than five minutes a barrage of abuse would be waiting for me when I got in the car.

'I've got better things to do than wait around for you,' he said. 'They only pay you to eight, so you should leave at eight.'

That wasn't the case, but I never corrected him. *He* was right, after all. I just tried to get my till area cleared up and my money cashed up before 7.50, so I could have the floors swept by eight and then leave.

One evening Mother called me into the lounge. Both parents were there waiting to speak to me. You're fifteen, I said to myself, only a year to go and then you'll be out. These 'chats' will be no more.

'You need to start paying rent,' Mother said. 'We can't afford to keep ya any more.'

After that, they took £20 a week off me. It didn't bother me. It actually made me feel more grown up and I knew that, if you had a job, you had to pay your way. It didn't end with rent, however. I had to start buying my own shampoo and body wash. I even had to buy my own crisps and biscuits and, though they still didn't allow me to touch their food, it didn't stop them from digging into my goodies. And my siblings had a good feast at my expense.

Meanwhile, new neighbours moved in. Alf, an elderly wheelchair-bound man who lived on the other side from the Bakers had died and his wife, May, had died a couple of years earlier. I used to close his curtains and make him a cup of Horlicks in the evening. He told me to stop coming when he found out that the money he was paying my parents wasn't getting to me. I'd assumed I was doing it for free, which I didn't mind at all. It was only a five-minute job, and I made the most of those few minutes out the house. Alf had asked what I was spending my money on. I hadn't a clue what he was talking about, so I didn't think about it. When he died, my parents didn't send flowers or even pay their respects when the funeral cars pulled up. They were too busy wrapped up in each other and their own selfishness. I suppose it was better than when Alf's wife died and Mother stood on the doorstep watching the funeral cars with a cigarette hanging out of her mouth. Alf's family looked at Mother in shame, but she didn't care. She talked so loud her voice echoed in the street full of silent mourners.

After I moved back home from Wendy's, Jack started coming over to our house again. I soon found out he had a crush on me. He had left school and started a new job. After his first week the lads took him out and got him so drunk that when he got out of the taxi, instead of going home, he came to our house. I was in bed, but I heard the hammering on the door.

'Col!' he shouted through the letterbox. I ran to the top of the stairs but Dad opened the door.

'I want Col,' he slurred. 'I love Col. Let me take her out.'

My parents found the whole situation hilarious and took him round to his own house. They often ridiculed me about having boyfriends.

'You're a dirty lesbian,' Mother said. 'No man's ever gonna want you.'

Dad said: 'You're never leaving the house so you'll never meet anyone anyway.'

Such an attitude meant they took me by surprise when one night they asked a neighbour of ours, Theresa, to babysit my siblings because they were taking me to the club.

I put on my best clothes, fixed my hair and waited for the taxi. As we walked in, the doorman stopped me. Dad whispered something in his ear and he waved me through.

We entered a smoky room that reeked of stale beer. Other members of my family were there, including my cousins. As I sat down I asked Mother why the doorman had stopped me. She shrugged her shoulders and, when Dad came back from the bar, she asked him.

''Cause she's black and they're not allowed in here, but I've sorted it. She's all right now.'

I felt my cheeks flush red. Everyone around the table heard him and all eyes were on me. I straightened up in my seat and started scanning the room, pretending I hadn't heard what my dad had just said and making out like I was excited.

It was a cabaret night and different acts came on to the stage – comedians, singers, magicians – but it was all a bit boring really. I tried to amuse myself by ripping beer mats. Mother kept disappearing and coming back, then disappearing again. A first I didn't pay much attention to her but then she introduced me to a boy named Steve. He was good-looking, but not my type – not that I really knew what was my type.

Dad piped up: 'When you takin' her out then?'

I wanted the ground to open up and swallow me. Without anyone consulting me, a date was set for the following weekend.

The next week, Steve turned up on my doorstep.

We were going to the cinema to watch *The Last of the Mohicans*. I asked my parents for some money.

'It's a date,' Mother said. 'It's his job to pay.'

We walked to the bus stop in silence. There were no pleasantries. As the bus headed towards our stop I started to panic. I pulled my coat pockets inside out and lied that I'd forgotten my purse. Steve smiled, and ushered me on to the bus.

We started talking about my school. I knew his brother and made a comment about them not looking alike. I asked if he had a different dad, like me. He told me he was adopted and that he didn't know who his parents were. They hadn't wanted him as a child and he'd been lucky to be placed with a family that did. I acted like I didn't know about foster parents or care. He thought I had a lovely family and he was so nice I didn't want to scare him off by telling him what they were really like.

After the film we waited again for the bus, once more in silence. What did I have to talk about? My life was boring, and after that night I was sure I wouldn't see him again. We got back to my street and he walked me to my door.

He leant in for a kiss, but I turned my head so he caught me on the cheek.

'Can I see you again?' he said. I nodded and went into the house. My parents were full of questions, but I just wanted to go to bed. I really liked Steve, but I didn't want to be his girlfriend. I didn't want a boyfriend. I was too busy trying to form a plan to get out of the house, and boyfriends were the last thing I needed. Eventually, he got the hint and moved on to a girl who moved into the street.

It was around this time that my granddad passed away. He'd been ill for some time and before I'd turned fifteen had been admitted to hospital. Finally, he succumbed to heart failure. My nan was inconsolable. I also felt a part of me die with him. He had helped raise me, and was more than just a grandparent.

And as if that wasn't enough to contend with, Wendy then moved in with us. She had been having trouble with her boyfriend so my parents let her stay.

We all attended my granddad's funeral but in the immediate aftermath it felt like life had changed for ever. On Sundays, we used to go to Nan's for visits with the rest of the family, but after Granddad's death that stopped. My aunties were still around to help Nan, but there didn't seem to be any more family get-togethers.

Wendy kept her flat on while she lived with us and so, every Friday, she met me from work and we would get a bit of shopping and make our way to hers.

My parents lightened up a bit when she moved in. They let me stay up a bit later. Wendy came with me to the park. She didn't behave like an adult; she was like one of us. She taught me how to apply make-up and told me about fashion. She also bought me my first alcoholic drink.

Wendy's flat was opposite an alleyway, where in the

evenings young lads would congregate. Wendy knew them all and often stood on her doorstep talking to them. She said they kept an eye on her flat when she wasn't there. She never let them in, though. She knew I was uncomfortable around strangers. The lads used to shout up the stairs to her flat, but I didn't reply.

One evening, Wendy wanted to go out and started throwing clothes from her wardrobe on to the bed. I thought she wanted to go to the bingo, but she laughed at me. She sorted out some clothes for me to wear, fixed my hair and did my make-up. Then she got ready herself. We both looked good and I felt good, but I was still unsure about where we were going. We jumped on the 65 bus, excited about what the night might bring. At the back of my mind I was worried, however. I couldn't stop thinking that the last time Wendy took me out my dad took me away. I didn't want to lose her again.

'He won't find out,' she said, laughing, as she pulled me out of my seat to get off the bus.

We were in the middle of Newtown, walking up the long road in tiny skirts and chiffon blouses. We stopped at a huge grey building, with 'Quasar' written down the side in big neon lights. The club was in the same building.

Pushing the big glass doors open, I could hear music. I didn't know what song it was; it was just a thumping beat. As we walked in, the sound of the music deafened me while the flashing lights blinded my eyes. I followed Wendy to the bar and she handed me a bottle and went off to find a seat. As I walked across the dance floor, huge men grabbed me, pulling me back to dance. I turned away and carried on following Wendy. We found a seat and, in my excitement, my drink went down my throat like water.

I found my shyness was slowly disappearing as I stood up and started dancing. I got lost in the music, dancing without a care in the world.

I felt like me – not a beaten or abused child. Just me.

The night went so quickly that when the lights came on I asked Wendy what was happening.

'It's time to go home,' she said.

I pulled myself up off the seat, but the room started spinning. I felt myself wobble, and a pair of arms caught me. I looked up and saw the sweetest smile I had ever seen. It was a boy, and the flash of his blue eyes brought me to my senses. I straightened myself up and pushed him away.

His name was Gary, he told me, and he worked in Quasar, next door. He asked if he could see me again, but I just stood there, staring at him, speechless.

'We'll be back here next week,' Wendy said.

And we were. The next month we went back every weekend. On Thursday nights I sorted out my clothes and Wendy would pack the bag.

Whenever we went back there I met Gary, and the more I got to know him, the more I liked him. He became my boyfriend, but I never told anyone about him, only Wendy. I only saw him on Friday nights, so there wasn't much to tell. I couldn't tell my parents about him because they didn't know that me and Wendy were going out.

On Saturdays I went to work and headed back to Wendy's when I finished. She cooked my dinner and we'd have a girlie night. We'd paint our nails, apply face packs, do waxing, scoff chocolates and drink Coke. We'd fall asleep on the sofa watching a film and would wake the next morning with cramp or a crick in our necks.

On Sundays we collected our stuff together and went back to my parents' house. I still had my chores, which I had to do if I wanted to carry on going to Wendy's flat.

Wendy now paid my rent. She paid Dad hers on a Friday, like I did, but because I was going straight to her place, she would pay for both of us and tell him she'd get the £20 back off me. She never did, though. She thought it was wrong that I had to pay rent and pay for my own toiletries and treats, so we came to an agreement. She would pay my rent and I would buy the first drink at the club. I had to be careful how much money I spent, though. If I spent too much on a Friday night my parents would ask where my money was. Once I told them I'd spent it on sweets and chocolate, but they saw right through me. Wendy slipped money in my purse and made out that I'd counted it wrong.

One Friday evening at the club Gary asked if he could come back to the flat. I immediately got nervous. I knew what he wanted. Although still fifteen, I was one of the few girls in my year at school that was a virgin.

At the end of the night as Wendy, Gary and I waited outside for a taxi, I felt sick. I wasn't ready. I wanted to end the relationship rather than deal with this.

In the taxi, Gary and Wendy laughed about the night, about how people dressed and danced. I was frantically working out ways to end it with him without letting him know the reason why. I didn't want him to think I was frigid.

Should I say something before we got out of the taxi? Should I wait until later? What would he say? Was he going to hate me and call me names?

When we pulled up outside the flat I grabbed the keys and ran straight up the stairs to the bathroom. I locked the door and sat on the edge of the bath, rocking back and forth, waiting. I could hear them both coming up the stairs. Wendy was calling me, asking what I was doing.

I could hear her directing Gary to the lounge while she went into the kitchen to make some coffee. I crept in behind her, trying not to let Gary see me.

'Get rid of him,' I said.

'You need to tell him the truth, babe,' Wendy said. We sat and drank coffee and continued talking into the very early hours. Every time Wendy got up to go to bed I stalled her by asking stupid questions.

'What we doing tomorrow?'

'What we gonna do when we get home?'

Eventually, Wendy cottoned on to what I was doing and took herself off to bed. She left her door open, though, because she knew how scared I was and, deep down, I think she was worried and wanted to be able to hear me if I needed her.

As we sat on the sofa, Gary folded his arms around me. I couldn't move my arms and I felt restricted. I panicked and pushed him away. Then I stood up and started sorting out the pillows and blanket, because the sofa was to be our bed for the night.

Gary stood and started stripping down to his boxer shorts. I had slipped on some tracksuit bottoms while I was in the bathroom. He grabbed my arm and pulled me close and started kissing me. I responded. It didn't feel that bad. I was fine with this.

We fell on to the sofa but everything was still good. We carried on kissing, stopping only to catch a breath. Then his hand started to pull on the waistband of my bottoms. My body went rigid.

'Relax,' he said, but I couldn't.

I jumped up.

'I'm on my period,' I blurted out.

I wasn't but I was so scared to say no that I said the first thing that came to mind. Gary stared at me, his eyes narrowing. He knew I was lying. He grabbed my hand and led me towards the sofa. He sat down and I sat next to him. My hands clenched together, sweating. He started to kiss me again and we lay down gently.

I couldn't do this. I pulled away. His grip around my waist got tighter.

'I can't,' I whispered. He loosened his grip. I turned my back on him and pretended to be tired. He pulled the blankets over us and lay close to me with his arm holding me like a protector. I could feel his breath on my ear. It was getting deeper and louder. I waited.

I looked round, knowing he had fallen asleep, and crept from underneath his arm and the blanket. I grabbed the dressing-gown from the back of Wendy's bedroom door and fell asleep on the chair. In the morning I said to Gary: 'I got up to go to the toilet and there was no room to get back on the sofa. I didn't want to wake you, that's why I was on the chair.'

After a coffee and pleasantries, Gary left. Wendy wanted to know everything but didn't look shocked when I told her nothing had happened. She just hugged me, for a very long time.

That day we decided to chill out. I called in sick to work and Wendy and I lounged about in our scruffs. We cleaned the flat from top to bottom, then we each had a long, hot soak in the bath. Bubbles were falling over the side, soaking the bathroom floor. It was bliss. As I lay there, steam filling the room and sweat dripping down my face, I thought about Gary. Was I being frigid? Why couldn't I relax? I started to get angry with myself and couldn't fight back the tears that I had kept so long at bay. Why wasn't I normal? My friends had managed to lose their virginity without being all upset about it. I wanted to have that closeness with someone.

I believed Gary cared about me, but that wasn't enough. I didn't know what I was looking for, but Wendy told me I'd know when the time came and the person was right.

'There's no hurry,' she said.

'Try telling my friends that,' I said.

I felt I was doing the right thing, but at the same time I hoped my decision to hold off wasn't going to be one I would regret.

13

That evening Wendy and I walked down to the shops. It was only five minutes away and, as we hadn't left the flat all day, the fresh air felt good.

I put Gary to the back of my mind. I'll phone him tomorrow, I thought. I wanted to enjoy my weekend before I had to go home.

We bought the usual goodies – sweets, crisps, pop. We even went to the chip shop and bought 'chips and curry sauce special'. Coming out, we bumped into the young lads Wendy knew from her road – the ones who hung around the alleyway outside her flat. We stood there talking to them for about ten minutes. They were on their way to a pub just a short walk up the hill.

As we walked off I literally bumped into a lad I knew from my school. He was coming out of the shop as I walked past, and I banged into him. His name was Kieran, and he was in my year.

'Sorry,' we both said, giggling when we recognized each other.

He was with a group of friends. As I scanned the group I noticed another lad I knew from school, called Aaron. We had gone to primary school together and had always got along really well. He was a nice person, not one of the lads that loved themselves and expected girls to fall over them all the time. He was genuine.

They started walking with us as we crossed over the main road and headed towards the flat. I had Kieran on my left and Aaron on the right. I looked back to see Wendy surrounded by the other lads. I hung back and waited for her.

I looked ahead at Aaron and Kieran. Aaron was grabbing Kieran's arm as if trying to slow him down. Wendy caught up with me and hooked her arm in mine. She started to push me towards the road. I started to panic. I just knew she was scared, I don't know how.

We crossed the second main road without telling the group but, slowly, they followed us. This time they were all spaced out. They had pulled their hoods up and had their hands in their pockets. Aaron had gone. He had carried on walking when we crossed over. The lads kept looking at each other and laughing.

'They're talking back-slang and I can't understand them,' Wendy said.

We picked up our pace. As soon as we turned the corner we didn't look back. We didn't say a word but we both knew we wanted to get home as quickly as possible.

We reached the corner of Wendy's road and glanced back. There was no one. It was dark and quiet. We looked at each other and let out a nervous giggle. We unlinked our arms and walked the short distance to the flat. Wendy had the door key so I followed her up the path to the front door. She opened it and walked in.

Her flat was quite small. As soon as you walked in there was a tiny hallway, and the stairs were right in front of you. Her front door had been sticking lately, because the wood had expanded during winter and you had to slam it to shut it, which rattled the whole house and annoyed the neighbours. As I was last in, I swung the door shut, kicked off my trainers and followed her up the stairs. But I can't have shut it properly.

At the top of the stairs, the door on the left led to the bathroom and ahead to the left was the lounge. A door to the right led through to the bedroom and the kitchen was on the right. Both the kitchen and bathroom could fit only one person at a time and the lounge couldn't fit any more than four comfortably. Wendy had a two-seater sofa and a chair, and that was it: practically all the space taken. There was just room for her little portable television in the corner, next to her stereo.

We went straight into the lounge and collapsed on to the sofa, hearts beating so fast we could hear each other's. We tried to work out what the boys had been saying in their back-slang language but gave up trying after about five minutes as nervousness turned to laughter. This was our last night before we had to go back home and we weren't going to let immature little boys ruin it. We both stood and headed towards the kitchen.

From there everything happened so quickly.

Just as we reached the lounge door there was a bang. We stared at each other then made for the top of the stairs.

I didn't get that far.

Someone pushed me into the lounge doorframe, the centre of my back bearing the brunt of the force. I heard Wendy screaming but I couldn't see her.

I caught a whiff of a man's deodorant, but all I could see were hoods. Four bodies pushed me into the bedroom and on to the bed. My arms were hoisted above my head and gripped tightly.

I looked up and saw Kieran. I tried to scream but a rough-skinned hand was covering my mouth. I couldn't breathe.

I started gagging, as laughter filled my ears. Suddenly the bedroom door flew open. It was Wendy, but she was being pulled back. I saw the rest of the lads who had been talking back-slang to each other earlier.

A body fell on top of me. I could feel hands reaching inside my tracksuit bottoms. I kicked out, but then hands were gripping down on my ankles. He got off and started pulling down my bottoms and underwear. He also had tracksuit bottoms on and pulled them down to his knees. Then he raped me.

He wasn't the only one who wanted 'a go' but, as quick as it happened, it ended. One penetrated me but didn't go any further.

Either way, they took something I had been holding

on to until the right time. These animals took my right away from me. They had taken something so special, after all my years of pain and abuse.

I felt a part of me die. In that moment I knew my life was never going to be 'normal' or 'sane'. It felt as though every last ounce of fight I had left was ripped from me.

14

We didn't sleep. We couldn't. I sat in the lounge while Wendy sat on the floor in the bedroom. She had thrown the quilt and sheets out of the bedroom window. She left the window wide open all night. We were numb. The cold weather was nothing.

At about seven thirty the next morning we walked back home. I was in pain as well as shock, so it took longer than usual.

Dad had just got up by the time we got back thirty minutes later. He didn't ask why we were home early and we weren't about to volunteer the reason. It wasn't something we had even decided between us. It just didn't feel right.

I really wanted my mother – or whatever it was a mother represented. Someone to hold me, to wrap me up in her love and protect me.

But my mother was not that sort of person. I couldn't even have a conversation with her. There were two ways she would react to something like this. Either she would erupt, take over the situation and demand blood – not from the perpetrators but from Wendy. I had been in her care, after all. Or, she wouldn't believe us.

The rest of the day went by in a blur. Friends asked

me several times if I was OK, but I appeased them with a nod of the head and a false smile. I didn't want to talk to anyone. If I started to speak I feared I would crack. My emotions and feelings didn't matter to anyone. Just shut up and deal with it, Collette, I told myself.

I went home and did my chores, sorted out my school uniform, finished off the last bits of homework and, after my siblings were bathed, had the longest, hottest soak ever. I topped up the tepid water with the hot tap very slowly.

If Mother had heard it she would have slapped me – and I knew how a slap on wet bare skin stung. I lay in the water, not knowing whether to drown myself or cry.

Eventually, I cried.

My whole body ached and I was bleeding below. I cried for what I had lost and what I had never had. Now I wished I had lost my virginity to Gary that Friday night. Maybe then last night wouldn't have hurt so much.

Mother walked in to use the loo.

'What you cryin' for?' she said.

'I'm not. It's just soap in my eyes,' I said, not that she cared why they were red and puffy. I got out and dabbed myself dry. I wanted my bed. I was exhausted. I hadn't spoken to Wendy all day, so now going to bed at the same time was going to be awkward. I knew she felt guilty. The look on her face every time I caught her glancing at me said it all. There was nothing to say, though.

It was my fault. I should have made sure the front door was locked shut. I was last in. It was my job. I didn't blame her.

I lay in bed staring up at the ceiling. I couldn't see anything because it was pitch black. It had been ever since my parents had removed the light bulb, telling me I wasn't allowed one.

I sang songs softly in my head, so I wouldn't think.

I don't know when I fell asleep, I just remember Wendy shaking me. She was crying. The bedroom door was open and the landing light was too bright for my eyes. I pulled the quilt back and moved over, thinking she was trying to get into bed. Instead, she was tugging my hand.

'Get up,' she said.

I sat up, eyes trying to adjust to the light, mind trying to fathom what was going on. I pulled on my dressing gown and slippers and followed her down the stairs.

As I walked into the lounge I could hear crackling from a radio. I peered around the door and there sat a policewoman. I almost fell over with fear. Thoughts raced through my head.

Wendy has told everyone. I'm going into care or, worse, prison. I felt like a little girl again. The room started to spin. I fell on to the arm of the sofa. Dad grabbed me and pulled me down on to the chair.

I glanced at Mother. There was a look of disgust on her face. It was as if I were a stranger to her. She didn't want to be in the same room as me. The officer stood up and started to gather her paperwork.

'We will be talking tomorrow,' she said, looking straight at me.

I nodded. My parents walked to the front door with her and were speaking in hushed voices. I looked at Wendy. She put a finger to her lips, warning me to be quiet. Mother came in, ahead of Dad.

'Dirty slut!' she spat as she walked past me on her way to the kitchen.

'You're a lying, sneaky little bastard,' Dad said, pointing his long finger in my face so his nail poked my skin under my eye. Mother ordered me back to bed from the kitchen. Dad walked off and sat on the sofa.

I went back upstairs, climbed into bed and lay there, confused. Was I dreaming? What the hell had just happened? This time, I waited for Wendy. I felt like I was going mad.

Wendy told me she had broken down in front of my parents and told them everything. Well, a version of the truth, anyway. She hadn't told them what really happened, because she was scared of what Mother would do to her.

I was scared about going to the police. They could take me away. I went along, at first, with Wendy's story. She told my parents about us going out, but that we had been broken into and that I had been held down while the lads robbed the place. She told them I had been touched up badly in the process but she couldn't help me because she was being held too.

She didn't tell them I was raped. Why?

I couldn't call Wendy a liar. She had always been there to help me but she was so scared of Mother.

When my parents quizzed me the following morning I confirmed everything she had said.

'You deserve to be touched up,' Mother sneered. 'Wearing such skimpy clothes. You're asking for trouble. Bloody cocktease.'

I tried to tell her I'd been wearing tracksuit bottoms and a T-shirt, but she wouldn't listen. She was convinced I had been wearing the clothes I had worn when I was sneaking off to the club. I think she was angrier because I was going out clubbing and she wasn't. Mother didn't really have many friends. This is why I think she was angry. We had been going out, enjoying ourselves. Mother only went out with Dad. She had no one else.

The following day I went to school. I saw Kieran and Aaron in their usual spot in the playground. Aaron scurried off, but Kieran gave me a knowing smirk. Again, I told no one and carried on as if the day was like any other. I had some lessons with Kieran, but avoided eye contact, making sure I was in the row in front. That way he could only see the back of my head.

In the dining hall, however, Aaron cornered me.

'It wasn't me,' he said. 'Please tell them it wasn't me.'

I knew he wasn't there, but he knew what his friends were going to do. Why didn't he warn us? Why did he leave them to it? Why didn't he phone the police? He may not have been involved, but he was still part of it as far as I was concerned. I didn't want to hear his pleas.

Friends asked me what was going on. I told them I'd seen Aaron that weekend and we were talking about what happened, just having a laugh. I kept that pretence up all day.

At the police station, however, it was a different story. I decided I would tell them everything. Dad came with me and waited outside as the interview started. He was clearly itching to know what I was saying because, after a few minutes, another officer came in saying my dad was demanding he be allowed to sit in. He'd said because I was under age I shouldn't be interviewed on my own. I knew he just wanted to know what was being said and so did the officer. I begged her not to let him in and said if she did then I wouldn't say any more.

Unfortunately, Dad was right. I was a minor and the law required an adult to be with me. The police said if I didn't want my dad then they could get a social worker to sit with me. That set off alarm bells. I didn't want to go back to care. I opted to retract everything I said and demanded to leave.

A female officer gave me a sympathetic look as she handed me my jacket and escorted me back to the front office of the station. There was Dad, pacing up and down like a prowling wolf. He tried to question me but I kept to the same story I had told him that morning.

If the police weren't going to help me, what chance did I have?

15

We didn't stay at Wendy's again. We did continue to go out, however. My parents were fine with it – as long as I paid for it myself and Mother came with us. The club to where Wendy and I had been going was closing down, as was Quasar, which meant I wouldn't be seeing Gary again.

That aspect didn't concern me very much because, since that weekend, I'd kept my distance from him. I had only called him once or twice since the night I was attacked. I think he got the message, because when I'd seen him in the club and he tried to approach me at the bar, I turned away from him. He had asked if I wanted a drink, but I couldn't look him in the eye. I turned my back and walked away. I felt awful. I was being a bitch, but I didn't want him near me, not even to talk.

I didn't hate men. I just didn't like them. In my mind, they only wanted one thing from a girl, and if you said no they took it anyway. In the immediate aftermath it felt like everything I had had been stripped away. I had no pride, no spirit, nothing. My existence was becoming a waste. Alcohol helped somewhat. It broke down my walls and allowed me to dance. Whenever I heard a beat, I wanted to dance. I could get lost in the words;

sing along like I was the only one in the room, not caring that people were watching me. They didn't know me – let them say what they wanted.

We started going to a different pub next to Quasar. It was a little, dingy bar, very old on the outside and dark and gloomy on the inside, but every Friday night a DJ played and the place was packed out. It was full with people of all ages, although the old ones hung around the bar while the younger crowd danced the night away.

Gradually, Wendy, Mother and me started meeting a few people in there, girls and lads, and I found it was possible to have fun again, dancing around the bar with bottles in our hands. As old and dingy as the pub was, it was also warm and inviting. Charlie Chaplin used to drink there, apparently. There were bars on the windows now, but it was a brilliant place. Hanging out there, I started to feel there was more to life again.

Most nights we walked on to a club afterwards, to a place ten minutes down the road. It was a tiny nightclub situated above a pub. The dance floor couldn't hold more than fifty people and it was dark and moody but we loved it. Again we met new friends in there too.

As far as Dad was aware, Mother came with us for the whole night, but after a while she stopped coming to the same pub as us. She went to one across the road. Then she met us later at the little club.

She was supposed to be the one keeping an eye on me but one night it was me who went over to the other pub to make sure she was OK. I walked in and saw her sitting at a table with a man I didn't recognize. His hands were all over her and the look on her face told me she loved it. When I approached the table Mother didn't look shocked to see me. She told me to pull up a chair. While the bloke she was with went to get me a drink I questioned her about her actions.

'Just having fun, Col,' she said.

She said she was just using this man for free drinks. When he returned, Mother introduced us. His name was Don and he was Irish. It was clear Mother hadn't told him she was married. He thought she was a single parent and gave me five pounds towards school pencils. I took it, but I didn't agree with what she was doing.

What could I do? If I told Dad, he would put an end to our nights out. It was the only source of fun I had. I wasn't going to let her ruin it for me, so I ignored what was going on. On other nights she brought Don to the club with us, but we never spoke to him. Wendy and I stayed on the dance floor.

Although I was having fun, I always watched what I was drinking. I felt like I had to be on my guard all the time. I never fully relaxed, no matter how much fun I was having.

The nights out did achieve one unexpected thing, however. Mother and I started speaking to each other, like friends do. We actually laughed. Could this be us finally getting closer together?

No.

The following morning, after the beer had worn off,

we went back to being strangers again. I clung on to that one night of the week, though. It kept me going until the following week.

One evening, a few weeks later, Wendy and me had been chilling in the park as we usually did during the week. When we got home I couldn't be bothered to sit around outside, so I went straight in and put my pyjamas on. Wendy came in not long after me and did the same. We were both so tired we went to bed and straight to sleep.

I woke to the sound of Dad shouting Wendy's name. We both sat upright in bed and looked at each other, confused. It was the middle of the night and everyone had been in bed sleeping. What could be so important?

Wendy went downstairs and I tried to go back to sleep. I was just dropping off again when the door was flung open and the landing light flooded the bedroom. I sat up and saw Wendy grabbing her overnight bag from the top of the wardrobe. She was crying and shaking as she filled it with her pyjamas, towels, underwear. When she had finished she got dressed. She was rushing, and I still didn't know what was going on. Wendy picked up her bag and headed towards the door. I was still waking up when she turned round and looked at me. She was pale, and her eyes were wide.

'They've got me a kidney,' she said. Then she left.

The following day my parents allowed me to go and see her in hospital, following her operation. She was hooked up to machines with wires and tubes everywhere.

She was still unconscious, but the surgery had gone really well. Now we had to wait. A family who had lost their baby son donated the kidney. Over time, Wendy's body accepted the new organ and when she was better she wrote a letter of heartfelt thanks to them. As she grew stronger, she didn't have to go for dialysis any more. I had never seen my auntie so happy. Finally, she had a chance to lead a normal life. Although her chances of having a family of her own increased with the transplant, she would have to undergo more surgery for that to happen.

Wendy came back to live with us and, one night, we were sitting on our usual place on the wall with some lads we knew and our neighbour Coleen when a car pulled up. It was a couple of older lads. One of our friends, Karl, went over to talk to them. The car pulled away after a while and, as I had to pick my little sister Audrey up from Girls' Brigade, we started to make our way across the park. I'd given up the brigade when Wendy moved in.

At the other end of the park the car we'd seen earlier pulled up again. I hadn't paid attention to the occupants before, but now I saw the driver. He was gorgeous. I had it in my head that he'd be interested in Coleen because she was really pretty and was always turning the boys' heads. So imagine how shocked I was when the cute lad jumped out of the car and threw himself at me. He blocked my way.

'I'm not budging till you tell me your name,' he said, smiling.

I was amused. I told him my name and age. He said he was called Mark and was eighteen.

'Do you want a gift?' he said.

'No,' I answered, getting a bit suspicious. I didn't know the man. All I knew was that he was a good-looking lad and he was interested in me. Coleen's face was a picture of pure jealousy.

'Where do you live?' he asked.

There was no way I could tell him that. My parents would go mad. To me, this was a grown man. It was a dream. I thought he only fancied me because he knew he couldn't have me. To get rid of him I gave him the name of my street but a different house number. I lived at number ten, and I said I lived at one hundred and ten. I didn't think my road was even that long.

The following day I told the girls at school but at first I don't think they believed me. I wasn't known for having boyfriends and no one really knew what I did at weekends. I sat and thought about my conversation with Mark all day during lessons, and he was all I talked about during break. I wanted to see him again but I knew there was no chance. I'd given him the wrong address for a start and, secondly, Dad would have none of it. Mark was way too old for me.

Back home, my parents were getting ready to go out. It was a warm evening and I was sitting in the front garden with Wendy, Coleen and Theresa. We were soaking up the last rays of the evening heat before it was time to go in. I sat on the doorstep and, stretching my legs out in front, closed my eyes and held my head back, feeling the sun warm my neck. As I dropped my head forward I saw a car, driving slowly as if the owner was looking for something. I strained my eyes and then I recognized the car. It was Mark.

I got up and ran into the lounge. I looked out the window and watched. Wendy and the others had clued on to what was happening and they followed me into the house. I giggled nervously. Was he looking for me? Surely not. My parents came down the stairs and asked what we were up to. Wendy blurted out: 'Col's got a boyfriend.'

I glared at her as she winked at me. She grinned as she told Dad how some lad was driving up and down the road because I had given him the wrong address. I waited for him to kick off. It went silent, then he said: 'Well, invite him round when we're here. I wanna meet him.'

Dad didn't seem to care that he was eighteen.

'Being your age, you're bound to have older relationships,' he said. I couldn't believe what I was hearing. Was this the same man who said I'd never be allowed to leave the house?

'I'll warn him to keep his hands to himself, mind,' Dad went on.

That didn't bother me. I was elated. I ran outside, but Wendy had beaten me to it. She had shouted to Mark to come back in an hour and, not knowing what was going on, he agreed.

When my parents went out I ran up the stairs,

brushed my hair, freshened up my make-up and changed my top. I sprayed perfume and body spray everywhere. I stopped and looked at myself in the mirror. What was I thinking? He won't be back, I thought. He just had time on his hands, that's why he was driving about. He wasn't really interested in me.

I was wrong.

On the hour, Mark pulled up outside, with the friend that was with him the night we had first seen him. The pal's name was Stuart and, after they'd come in for a few minutes, we realized they were both really nice lads. Stuart was one of the funniest people I had ever met. The two of them bounced off each other and soon had us all creasing with laughter. It was hard not to like them.

When Mark and I had five minutes on our own, he made fun of me for giving him the wrong address. I explained what my parents were like; he said it was understandable and thought it was my parents being protective. I called it controlling. He worked in a paint shop and we talked about my school. He knew a lot of the lads in my year, mainly through their brothers or sisters.

As the evening wore on, I started to panic because Dad had said Mark wasn't allowed at the house until he'd met him. If he came back and saw him, he'd kill him *and* me. We agreed on a time for him to come and see Dad and they said their goodbyes to everyone. The whole time we were together Mark held my hand, and when he was getting ready to go he pulled me over to the car with him. He drew me in close and cupped my face with his hands. I closed my eyes and waited. He kissed me so softly. I pulled him closer and kissed him back.

The following day I was on cloud nine. I couldn't wait to get to school and tell everyone. Laura and I were still best friends and we still walked to and from school together, but Debbie, Susan and Zara were 'the girls'. They all had boyfriends and had already lost their virginity. Where boyfriends were concerned, I had some catching up to do.

In class I closed my eyes and daydreamed about my kiss with Mark. I tried to remember every detail – his smile, his eyes, his smell.

At lunchtime a girl named Natalie came tearing across the playground, heading straight towards me.

'Some lad in a car is outside the gates looking for you,' she said, trying to catch her breath.

I headed towards the gate, not running – I wanted to look cool – but walking really fast. My heart was in my mouth. I got to the gate . . . and nothing. There was no one there. I went red, thinking he'd gone. He must have seen the uniform and thought I was ugly and left.

I wasn't allowed to wear make-up for school. Maybe that was it. Mark hadn't seen me without make-up on before.

BEEP.

I looked over to the shop where the sound came

from. And there was Mark's car. I ran over the road towards him, followed by 'the girls', all giggling like the schoolgirls we were.

'Hi, babe,' he said. It was his breaktime, so he thought he'd pop round to see me. The girls were questioning him about how much he liked me; it was like the Spanish Inquisition. I didn't care, though, I sat in the front passenger seat staring at him, his gleaming blue eyes and cheeky grin and clean blond hair. This was my boyfriend. I was gobsmacked.

That evening, I sat and waited nervously. Was Dad going to make a show of me? Was Mother going to start calling me a lesbian? Were they going to make fun of me?

'Your boyfriend's here,' Dad said.

I jumped up and opened the front door. I had already asked Mark not to say anything about coming round the night before, or about coming to my school. I had also told him about the warning Dad was going to give him. Mark just hugged me and told me not to worry.

When Mark came into the house, Dad shook his hand.

'She's only fifteen, so no funny business,' he said.

Mark had brought Stuart with him, and as I got to know them I saw how close they were. They always looked out for each and were more like brothers than friends. Mark managed to win Mother over by buying her a bouquet of flowers. She fell in love with him instantly.

Wendy had fallen for Stuart, even though he was younger than her. They got on really well. It was right for them to be together.

Mark and Stuart started coming out with us on Friday nights, meeting us in the pub before we all went on to the club together. They also took my dad to the pub on Sunday afternoons. The two of them quickly became a part of our family; they had even met my nan. My parents were slowly loosening the grip they had over me.

Mark spoiled me rotten. Whatever I wanted, I had it. He bought me my first pair of named trainers, he took me out for dinner, he babysat with me on weekends, he picked me up from school and work, and sometimes he would bring me a McDonald's at lunchtime. All my friends thought I was so lucky. They loved him, and the lads were jealous. I walked with my head held high: I was in a grown-up relationship. It felt like I had a second chance to decide the way my life was going to go.

A week before my sixteenth birthday, Mark and I were sitting in the car in the park while the others messed about at the swings. I looked at him, and he looked back. I wanted to freeze that moment. I didn't want to say what I was about to say, but I had to.

'I was raped,' I said quietly.

I will never forget the look on his face. I thought it was me shaking, but when I looked down I saw it was Mark. His hand gripped mine, his knuckles turning white. We sat in silence. As he wrapped his arms around me I collapsed, crumpling like paper.

I poured my heart out to him — about my parents, the rape, everything.

He listened as I described in detail what had happened that weekend. A sense of relief washed over me when I finished. We could see everyone coming towards the car. I got out and walked home. I needed some space.

For the first time ever I had opened up to someone about my personal life, my most private feelings. I know it was my idea to tell him but soon I felt confused. Was I about to push the only good thing in my life away because of old wounds? I didn't want to, but it was down to him now. If he didn't turn up tonight, I'd understand.

I needn't have worried. Mark did turn up, and when his car pulled up outside the house my heart flipped. I ran to open the door. He greeted me with a smile and a wink. I threw my arms around his neck and squeezed. All evening I sat so close to him you couldn't have slipped a sheet of paper between us. I needed to be close to him, I needed him to hold me. He knew my secrets and yet he was still here. He still loved me. As the evening ended and it was time for him to leave, I found myself gripping on to him. He pulled me away and asked what was wrong. I told him about my insecurities, how I hadn't thought he was going to turn up. He stopped smiling and held me close. I could feel his heart beating through his top as I took in the smell of his aftershave. I had butterflies. I knew what I wanted.

On Friday I went to work as usual, but with a spring in my step, thinking about my sixteenth birthday. Mark said he wanted to treat me. I was all excited and in love. When I got there I filled up the cigarette racks, and as I did I heard shouting coming from the aisles. I didn't really pay any attention, though. For one thing, I was in my little bubble of happiness which nobody was going to burst, and for another, it was coming up to closing time and the lads who worked in the warehouse out the back often messed about, chucking toilet rolls at each other, dancing with brooms and racing shopping trollies.

BOO!

I jumped and turned round, expecting to see one of them. I was about to let off a barrage of abuse at whoever it was for scaring me . . . then I froze. It wasn't the lads from the warehouse messing about. It was the lad who raped me.

I screamed, and the manager came running out. He could see I was in a state but didn't know why. This lad just stood there, leaning on the counter, chewing gum and smiling at me.

'Get out,' my manager said, pulling him by his coat. When I looked out of the huge windows it was like my childhood nightmares all over again. All those lads were standing there, noses pressed up at the glass, pulling faces at me.

I looked beyond them and saw a car pull up, music blaring. It was Mark, arriving to pick me up. They all ran when Mark jumped out of the car. I'd told him who the lads were that night I said I'd been raped.

He ran into the store.

'You OK?' he said. I could hear the fear in his voice.

'Take her home,' my manager said.

We had barely made it to the car when I broke down, shaking with terror. As we started to pull off, Mark phoned Stuart. He was already at my house seeing Wendy. I tried to calm down, wiping the tears away, straightening myself up, when Mark slammed on the brakes. I looked up, and we were parked in Erdington cemetery, music still blaring, engine still running but car door wide open. Mark was gone. He was running off in the direction from which we had just come. I switched off the engine, and elderly ladies started coming out of the church, wondering what all the commotion and noise was. I tried to apologize but, understandably, they were concerned. They wanted me to move the car, but I couldn't get the words out to tell them that I couldn't drive. Then Mark came back. He apologized to the ladies and we sped off towards home.

He said that he'd spotted one of the lads and chased him into McDonald's. He had gone behind the counter and the staff had protected him, not letting Mark get to him. They threatened to call the police, so Mark left it.

I had never seen him so angry. The speed he was driving was scary. I gripped on to the door handle as we flew round corners, and we screeched to a stop outside my house, where Stuart was waiting. I got out, but the engine was still running. I looked at Mark.

'Don't, Col,' he said.

With that, Stuart got in and they drove off. Mark didn't come back that night, and I didn't sleep. I lay awake, wondering where he was. Wendy couldn't get in touch with Stuart either. We were both more than worried.

My manager gave me the following day off. He had phoned my parents and said there had been an incident at work the night before and I was to stay home to rest. My parents never asked what had happened. I don't think they cared.

I was constantly up and down to the window, waiting for Mark to pull up. I knew he was at work but that didn't stop me. The time went by so slowly. I picked at my dinner. My parents got ready to go out – again. My mind was on Mark. Coleen came round and asked if she could hang out at our place that night. I said I didn't mind. Really, I didn't care.

'Mark's here!'

I don't know who shouted it. All I know was that I ran out to him and stopped in my tracks as he got out of the car with a huge bouquet of flowers and a flash of his cheeky grin. Part of me was angry with him for leaving without saying a word, but the other part was happy that he was OK.

We didn't talk about what happened the night before. I didn't want to know. Wendy found out, though. She went on and on at Stuart until he gave up and told her. They had gone outside to talk – they were out there ages; I thought they were having some 'alone' time. When they came in, Wendy called Mark into the kitchen. They were only gone a couple of minutes before they came back in.

Wendy threw something in my direction. I ducked, and heard a jangling sound as something fell to the floor behind me. I looked over the back of the sofa, and there were her keys to her flat. Mark went and picked them up and took me out to the car. We got in, and Mark asked how I felt about going to Wendy's flat. I knew how I felt. It was something I really didn't want to do.

Wendy had wanted to go back to her flat again but so far I had said no. She could go back if she wanted but I couldn't even go past the road in the car or on the bus without feeling physically sick. Each time I went near my stomach lurched like I'd been punched.

Mark tried to convince me there was nothing to be scared of. He said he would be with me every step of the way and if I wanted to leave I could. He said I had to be strong against bullies, not to allow anyone to take away my freedom. I relented and we drove off in his car.

We pulled up outside and I sat in the car, my head down. I just couldn't look up. It was like a horror film: I was scared of what I might see.

Mark opened the car door and helped me out. Still looking down, I let him guide me towards the front door. He lifted my chin with his hand and smiled. He then took hold of my hand and opened the door. I froze as I started to replay that night in my head. I could smell the lads' body odour and started to heave.

Mark went in first. I followed him and as I got in the door I turned, took hold of the door and, screaming, slammed it as hard as I could. I then lost it, punching and kicking the door until Mark pulled me back. He showed me the door was shut and locked it. We slowly made our way up the stairs, each step feeling steeper than the next and my legs shaking like jelly.

We got to the top and I pushed the bedroom door open with my finger. The bed was still stripped of bed-clothes. The cold air from the room hit me and I ran into the bathroom to throw up. Mark rubbed my back as I fell to my knees. I started to get angry. What right did those bastards have?

They had been arrested for breaking and entering but had escaped prosecution on the technicality that the door had been open. I hadn't shut it properly. The rape charge was a non-starter because of my refusal to give a full statement.

All the frustration of the last few weeks boiled over. I wanted to punch and kick something, anything, but I didn't have the strength. I had no energy left, not even to cry.

But then, suddenly, something came over me, like I was being taken over. I stood up. My anger seemed to conquer the fear. My legs no longer felt like jelly, my hands stopped shaking and the nauseous feeling subsided.

I walked into the lounge, over to the window. The street was quiet – no cars, no pedestrians, just a cat jumping from one garden to the next. I closed the curtains and walked towards Mark. He reached out for the light switch but I grabbed his hand. I leant in for a kiss and we fell into each other's arms. I started to undress him but he stopped me.

'I need to,' I said.

Mark laid me down and took what I had left. He was gentle and kept asking if I was OK, never once taking his eyes off me, stroking my hair as we rolled around on the floor.

It felt right. It was something I needed to do.

People may find it weird that I made love for the first time at the place I was raped but, as I lay in Mark's arms, I was conscious of the horrible flashbacks being erased by new memories – for that night anyway.

16

On the day of my sixteenth birthday I woke up feeling really excited. I had reached a milestone.

I ran downstairs. Dad was sitting on the floor in front of the fire, reading the newspaper. He didn't raise as much as an eyebrow as I entered. I walked through the lounge into the kitchen, where my brother and sister were sitting eating their breakfast. They didn't acknowledge me either.

I went into the bathroom and stared at myself in the mirror. It *was* my birthday, wasn't it? Was I sleepwalking? Had I got the wrong day? No, I hadn't. What was going on then?

Then I twigged. I must be having a surprise. What could it be? A party? A big, expensive present? Best just to go along with it. I went back upstairs to get dressed, giggling with excitement to myself. I started humming as I made my bed, opened the curtains and picked up Audrey's nightdress from the floor.

'Shut the fuck up!' Mother shouted from her pit. She had been out the night before and must have been nursing a hangover.

I danced down the stairs, shaking my hips back and

forth, thinking about how my party was going to look. I swooped into the lounge and, this time, Dad looked at me over the top of his glasses.

'Happy birthday,' he said.

'Thank you,' I replied, smiling as I gathered my stuff to leave for school. I started my walk to the bus stop. As I turned the corner, a car pulled up, music blaring. It was Mark.

We had become inseparable. Finally, I had a feeling I belonged to someone, and in a good way. Everything seemed to be going so well in my life. It felt like it was my turn to be happy and that I deserved it. I was going to marry Mark and have the life I'd always wished for.

'Happy birthday, babe,' he said. I got in and he drove me to school, picking up my friend Debbie on the way.

'What did your parents get you?'

'Nothing yet,' I answered.

He looked shocked.

'It's OK,' I said. 'I think they're planning a surprise party.'

His expression turned to one of confusion. Bit strange, I thought, but then I realized that the reason Mark didn't know anything was because my parents didn't trust him with the secret. I kissed him and went into school. We made plans to see each other at lunchtime, when he would take me to McDonald's. He'd meet me after school with his presents.

In school my friends gave me lots of cards and 'the

girls' even gave me a box of chocolates, which we sneaked during English.

After school I ran out to Mark's car. I couldn't wait to see what he had for me. His back seat was filled with flowers. They smelled beautiful but I had to wait until I got home to open the others. Outside the house he gave me my card – a big one with 'Girlfriend' splashed across the front. I thanked him with a kiss.

Walking into the house, I was overflowing with excitement, not sure what to expect. Slowly, I opened the lounge door, waiting for someone to jump out on me. I could hear the TV. I peered around the door. Mother was in the kitchen peeling the potatoes. Dad was in the same place I'd left him that morning, watching the TV. My brother and sister were upstairs getting changed out of their uniforms.

There were cards on the coffee table. I opened them. They were from my nan, my auntie Sue and her kids, and the Bakers.

There was nothing from my parents. My eyes started to fill up but I fought like mad to stop the tears falling on to my cheeks. I didn't want Mark to see how this bothered me. I didn't want it to. I didn't want to care that my parents didn't love me.

Mark had bought me a new coat, a top, a pair of jeans and a ring. The top and jeans were way too big for me. I made a joke to him about how fat he must think I was. We took them back to the shop but, when I couldn't find alternative sizes or styles, he gave me the money to buy something else.

When I recounted this to Dad after we got back home, he said, 'Give it to me. I'll look after it until you find something.'

I never saw that money again.

My flowers filled three big vases and instantly brightened the dimly lit lounge, providing a splash of colour against the smoke-stained walls and the grubby carpet, which looked like something out of a social club with its fag burns.

Wendy arrived later and gave me fifty pounds. She'd been spending less time at the house and her relationship with Stuart had come to an end, which meant I had hardly seen her of late. That night she announced to Mother she was moving back to her own place. She was back with her ex-boyfriend Tom.

I went to bed that night trying to convince myself I was happy with my lot, but something changed that day.

Over the following days and weeks I became tetchy. I started snapping at friends, starting arguments for no reason and once even fighting with one of them. At school I gave cheek to the teachers, arriving having not done my work, or without so much as a pen.

I would stand outside the school, on the opposite side of the road, and blatantly light up a cigarette. The teachers shook their heads at me, knowing they couldn't do anything, as I was old enough to buy them now.

I also started to cheek my parents. They still slapped me, but I would egg them on.

'I'm used to your beatings,' I said. 'You don't scare me any more.'

I even began closing myself off from Mark. I told him over the phone not to bother coming to the house, but he still showed up so I sent him away. I shouted at him on the doorstep in front of everyone, laughed in his face and felt proud of myself for making someone feel like crap.

He was like my puppy. No matter what I said or did he was still there, nipping at my ankles.

One night he turned up to collect me from work, but I wanted to catch the bus with my mate. Instead of explaining this to Mark or asking him to give her a lift, I started shooting my mouth off.

'You're such a stalker,' I said, when he arrived at the door with his usual smile. 'Get a life. You make my skin crawl.'

I made him look like a complete idiot in front of my colleagues who were leaving at the same time. Everyone stood in silence. I looked at my mate and started laughing. She just stared at me. I looked at my manager, who was pulling down the shutters. Even he looked taken aback.

They started walking off, leaving me standing on the high street on my own. The shops were closed and it was deadly quiet. I walked off in the opposite direction, the longest way to the bus stop, hoping to miss the next one.

I fished in my bag for a fag and a lighter and, having counted out the right change, stood there in the darkness waiting for the bus.

I saw Mark, in his car, watching me. I went over and opened the door.

'What you doin'?' I said.

'Making sure you get home OK,' he said.

He would have followed me all the way home if he had to.

'This person isn't you, Col,' he said. He said he was going to stay away for the weekend. 'You need a break,' he said.

I thought he was breaking up with me but, as he cupped my face, I knew he was doing this for me. My head was shot. I knew I needed some sort of help. With my exams coming up and Dad wanting me to go to college, relationships and work were the last things I needed. I had to study hard if I wanted to get into college. It was my only route to a good job and a passport out of this pig hole.

When it was time for my college interview, Dad came with me and answered their questions for me.

'She wants to be a children's nurse,' he said when the tutor asked about my goals.

No I didn't. I didn't know what I wanted, but I didn't want to be a nurse. The decision was made for me. He signed me up for my Tec in childcare, which, depending on my GCSE results, I would be starting in September.

My head felt like it was in a bubble. I could hear Dad and the tutor talking, but it was as if my vocal cords had been cut.

At home I tried so hard to pluck up the courage to tell my parents that I didn't want to be a nurse, but whenever I found the right time my mouth dried up. My mind started to play tricks on me and I forgot what I wanted to say. I got all tongue-tied. I babbled about how hard college was going to be, but Dad flew off the handle and accused me of being lazy, so I jumped up and made him a drink, leaving him to calm down. It was better to change the subject and go upstairs.

Dad came with me to my enrolment and gave my tutor our home telephone number, telling her to ring him if I was ever absent. He then went into the story about how he had caught me wagging school.

I really wanted to cry.

He started asking questions about homework and grants, promising the tutor that I would be a model student. I was screaming inside. I started to pinch myself and my legs started to shake. I didn't want to do this. I wanted to leave. I needed to get out. This was *my* future, but I had no say in it. I had to do as I was told and get on with it. My dream was to leave Birmingham. I wanted to have fun and some time to myself.

Before college began, Mark and I sat down and agreed to make our relationship work. I told him I would go to college and get a career while he worked and we would get our own home. It sounded so sensible, but something would set us off and we'd argue. We were getting on each other's nerves if we stayed around each other too long but, at the same time, we needed to see each other.

One day I was walking through Stockland Green when I saw my friend Susan, who had moved to Essex a week before our exams. I had heard she was back in Birmingham, but we hadn't met. We hugged and exchanged pleasantries. She asked what I was up to and she told me she'd got a job in a café. When she'd left our school she hadn't enrolled in another, so she hadn't done her exams. She didn't care, though. She loved her life.

She asked how Mark was and I could tell she was dying to tell me something. There was a sneaky look in her eye and she was shifting from one foot to the other.

'Oh, we've finished,' I said. We hadn't, but I wanted to know what she had to say.

'I slept with him,' she said.

She made out they had a drunken thing at a party Mark had thrown while his parents were away. I remembered that party. I hadn't been allowed to go but told Mark to have the party anyway. She went into detail about his house and bedroom, the colour of the carpet and his bed quilt cover. She even knew about my picture on his bedroom wall. All the time she was talking I could picture them together.

I needed to go. I didn't know where, and I didn't

care, I just had to leave this conversation. I walked off, head spinning. Susan was calling after me, but I didn't look back. My mouth filled with water as I grabbed hold of a wall, the feeling of nausea rising in my throat.

'Happy thoughts, happy thoughts,' I repeated over and over to myself, but, not feeling any better, I walked on. I headed to the park where I had first met Mark. I sat on the wall and remembered that sunny evening – playing football and pushing Wendy on the swings. A lot had happened in the eighteen months since that night. In such a short space of time everyone and everything had moved on.

That night I saw Mark and put to him what Susan had said. He protested his innocence.

'Everyone was everywhere in the house that night,' he said. 'Yes, Susan may have seen my bedroom, but so did lots of other people.'

Something inside me believed him. I knew deep down that he wouldn't hurt me, but something also told me I was better off on my own, and I ended it for good that night. Maybe, somewhere inside of me, I had been looking for the opportunity to end it.

So, I threw away my one chance at happiness. What did it matter? Good things were what happened to other people.

Dad was happy I was going to college. I just wanted to get on with things, and I hoped college would give me the respect I had been craving from my parents for sixteen years. Perhaps if I became a nurse they would show me off to their friends and, for a change, my siblings would be in my shadow.

I was turning seventeen, going to college and starting a new chapter in my life. I told myself things could only get better. They couldn't get any worse, could they?

17

The house was eerily quiet when I emerged from my bedroom one afternoon after college. Mother had already had a go at me for neglecting my chores, which had increased in intensity since I'd been forced to quit my Kwik Save job due to my ongoing kidney problems. Now that I had no money coming in, Mother had demanded I do even more about the house to compensate.

I was expecting another earful about how I wasn't pulling my weight as I went down the stairs, but I couldn't hear a sound in the rest of the house.

I pushed the living-room door open, preparing myself for the tongue-lashing. I just caught sight of her, sitting on the floor, grinning manically at me, when I felt it. An icy cold shock went right down my spine, swiftly followed by something banging off my head. The fright got me more than anything. Then I heard her cackle. Finally, I twigged. A bowl of cold water had been placed over the door, to fall on the next person through it. No prizes for guessing who'd put it there.

Mother was still laughing uproariously.

'That'll teach ya not to clean the bath as I told ya,' she said.

I ran back upstairs and dried myself off. I had to change my top, as the water had gone right down my back.

I suppose it was preferable to the slaps she'd been administering lately – across the face for cardinal sins like failing to clear the table when asked or not sorting out dinner as quickly as she wanted.

That night I prepared for my customary soak in the cold water left after my siblings had got out of their bath. I still had my clothes on and was about to add some hot water when someone grabbed me from behind.

Before I knew what was happening my legs were lifted from under me and I was in the water, still fully clothed. I yelped like an injured dog, the cold of the water assaulting all my senses at once, water splashing everywhere.

Mother's insane cackle echoed around the bathroom.

'And you can clean up the mess in here as well,' she said.

I dried myself off for the second time that day, tidied the bathroom and went straight to bed.

I was rudely awakened the next morning by the mattress being lifted up – while I was still on it. Mother tipped it right up so I fell down on to the bedframe.

'Get up, you lazy git,' she said. 'I want you to sort out your brother and sister before you piss off for the day.'

Was there no end to this humiliation?

With no money and no boyfriend, my social life was

non-existent. I was back to being a glorified cleaner and babysitter.

My only respite was my new college, and it was an eye-opening experience for me in one respect at least – I got to see how 'normal' families worked.

The other girls talked about going into Sutton Coldfield to the pubs and having a good time. I sat and listened. I might have been seventeen and embarking on a new chapter, but their lives seemed a world away from mine.

I grew weaker and weaker. I could actually feel my spirit sapping from me. I had nothing to look forward to. I'd been pushed down so many times that I'd become resigned to the fact that I'd never leave. Dad was right. I'd be stuck at home for ever.

My one consolation was that, at college, my new friends were lovely, well-spoken and well-dressed. They all seemed to come from beautiful big houses and loving families. They intrigued me. In a group of about six of us, I was the only one not to come from Sutton Coldfield. The others had known each other from secondary school, but they welcomed me into their company.

Most of them came from homes where both parents worked full-time and money seemed to be no object. One of the girls even had her own car, paid for by her parents. I wasn't jealous of their material wealth. Mother had been working as a dinner lady, and Dad was still a mechanic. They couldn't afford to buy me a car, even if they wanted to. What struck me, however, was how nice their families were. I could tell by listening to their stories that they were happy and always had been.

I couldn't imagine telling them stories about my family. I could never tell them my parents hated me, or that I was ashamed of them, because they were cruel, loud and brash, how they sank lager and bitter and binged on curries.

When one day our afternoon classes were cancelled, one of the girls, Sarah – the one with the car – offered to give me a lift home. She was so well-spoken that when she swore it sounded wrong. The last thing I wanted was for her to come home and meet Mother, with her foul tongue. I tried to ignore her, but she kept on.

In the car, I tried to make excuses for her to drop me off elsewhere, but Sarah said it was no trouble and she wanted to see where I lived. I could feel my face getting redder and hotter as we pulled up outside my house. I couldn't look her in the eye. I reached for the door handle as she switched off her engine, shouting, 'Bye!', but Sarah got out of the car too. She obviously wanted to come in for a coffee.

My hand was trembling as I pushed my key into the lock. Mother was still at work but just the thought of her being there made me feel physically sick. As we walked into the living room, the smell of stale cigarettes hit me. Mother hadn't even washed up the breakfast dishes before she went to work. Again, I felt my face burning up. I kept apologizing for the state of the house, saying Mother had to leave early for work. Sarah must have known I was lying.

As I made up excuses about the state of the furniture, I cleaned, washed up, vacuumed, polished and made a coffee. Just as I sat down to talk I heard the key in the door. My heart sank to my stomach. I felt cold, yet I was sweating.

In walked Mother. As soon as she saw Sarah, her mouth twisted. She went straight into the kitchen and banged cups together, slamming the kettle on to the worktop. Sarah and I sat in silence, but then she let out the tiniest nervous giggle.

The kitchen door swung open and there Mother stood in the doorway, white foam in the corners of her mouth.

'What's so fuckin' funny?' she said.

'Sorry,' I said. 'We'll be quiet.'

Mother wasn't done, however.

'What are you doing in my fuckin' house anyway?' she said to Sarah. 'Did I say you could come in? Get out, you dirty lesbian!'

Tears filled my burning eyes. I wanted the ground to open up and swallow me.

Sarah stood up and grabbed her bag. As she left, she gave me a hug. Mother ran into the living room. I stood between her and Sarah as she ran out of the door, down the path and into her car. Mother slapped me across the mouth and tore a handful of hair from my head.

I didn't go into college the next day. I just couldn't

stand the shame. As the days wore on, I went in again, but only for an hour, then I skipped the classes and walked around Sutton Park for the rest of the day.

I pretended I had tons of homework to do and lay on my bed thinking where I could go if I left, often crying myself to sleep because I knew I had no one. I was trapped. My life was going nowhere, and fast.

At night when I came in, I put on my pyjamas, often missing my tea, but Mother still called me down to do the washing-up. If she wanted fags from the shop, or even sweets for the siblings, she made me get dressed again and go out.

As for me, her attitude was 'No job, no luxuries.'

Being their errand girl was bad enough, but trips to the shops sometimes felt like running the gauntlet too. I became the target for older bullies who had moved into the street. There was one girl who really had it in for me. She called me 'Paki' and tried to get a rise from me, and if I stood my ground her older friends would join in too.

One night our stand-off came to blows and I returned home with a scratched face. I was in a bit of pain but was more worried about having taken too long at the shop. When I got back to the house I told Mother what had happened.

'You should've kept your gob shut,' Dad said.

My parents knew all about the bullying I was getting from those girls but, instead of helping me, they saw it as a way of beating me down again and, strange as it may sound, getting another house.

At this time, it had emerged that Birmingham City Council planned to tear down the houses in our street because they were falling apart. They had only been thrown up after the war and, because they'd been ear-marked for demolition, the council had refused to carry out repairs for years.

Mother and Dad were all over the situation, playing the system for all they could get. They refused to dec-orate, because the more out of date the house looked, the better the case against the council. They picked plaster from the walls, making holes, and poured water on the floorboards to cause damp. Every other day one of them would be at the doctor's complaining about damp-related ailments so they could claim more com-pensation. Mother was always on the phone to the council or the solicitor, trying every stunt in the book to be moved into another house.

When I had the fight, Mother was straight on the phone to the council, going on about racism.

One evening Mother was standing by the window, not even trying to hide the fact she was looking out for someone, her neck stretching to look over the bush in our front garden, her devious green eyes darting from one side to the other. After half an hour she told me to put on my coat and shoes. I obeyed, of course, but was shocked when she said we were walking to the shop.

For some reason, my nerves kicked in. I started to feel sick and my throat was so dry I couldn't swallow.

As we walked down the road my mind started to play tricks on me. Maybe my mother did care about me; maybe she was worried for my safety and wanted to protect me.

Mother walked with her hands in her pockets. It's not like she would ever hold my hand. Suddenly they shot out of her pockets and clenched. I looked up and saw the girl who was bullying me walking towards us. Mother had obviously seen her walk past our house earlier, so she knew we would bump into her. As we got closer to each other I could see the smile on Mother's face. I clenched my fists, but my heart was thudding so fast I thought it was going to pop out of my chest. Suddenly we were face to face, but it wasn't me the girl stared at, it was Mother.

They started shouting in each other's faces, spit flying from their mouths as they cussed each other with every swear word imaginable. It was embarrassing. Then the girl punched my mother. She had a knuckle-duster on her hand. Clearly, she had been waiting for me but was happy to deal with Mother instead.

Mother and the girl were really going for it, pulling at each other's hair and swapping punches. I stood back and watched for a moment, perversely revelling slightly in my mother getting her head kicked in for once. It gave me a strange sense of empowerment.

Whether I liked it or not, she was still my mother. I

pulled the girl off, but, as I did, Mother swung a punch and the girl fell to the ground. Mother spat on her as we walked off. She was seething, however.

'You should've kept out of it,' she said, before adding: 'It was your fight anyway. You're such a fanny having me fight your battles.'

She'd obviously forgotten I'd just saved her from having her head smashed in with a knuckle-duster. Dad got a different version of events – as did the police when they came round. Two weeks later, the council moved us into a bigger house that Mother had spotted standing empty.

If moving into that house had made me feel I was part of the family, moving out had the exact opposite effect. Once again I shared with my sister but, from the moment we moved in, my parents referred to that bedroom as *her* room. I felt I had to ask to go up to it and, once I started, asking permission to use it became a 'rule'.

Mother and Dad didn't allow me a key to the front door, they banned me from using the telephone and I had to ask for food. Even though they seemed delighted to have me around to do chores and babysit, I always felt I was on borrowed time.

I began to engage more at college and started a placement in a residential home, where I went twice a week. I loved it. I landed a weekend job there and worked during the holidays. I was earning money again but, once my bus pass, rent and toiletries were taken off, I didn't see much of it. Whatever I had, my parents 'borrowed' and I never saw it again. Dad checked the hourly rate and made sure he knew exactly how much money I had.

He also made me phone my manager to ask for a job for Mother. I didn't want her to work with me and I tried telling him there were no jobs, but Dad made me phone them in front of him and he heard my manager say yes.

I felt suffocated. No matter what I did or where I went Mother had to somehow be a part of it. I started going back to classes, to get away but also to have company. However, a thirst for learning was still not there, so I spent most of the time sitting outside the college with my friend Jenny, smoking and watching the world go by.

Jenny was so kind and sweet-natured; she spoke softly and was the one person since school that I felt I could talk to about my abusive relationship with my parents. I confided in Jenny and we would sit and talk for hours, either on the grass or in a doorway. Jenny was beautiful, tall with perfect skin and long red hair. Boys and men often stared and handed her their numbers. I never once felt jealous; I never felt like the 'ugly one'.

I became reacquainted with Trev, a lad in McDonald's who always gave me discounts on my lunches. Jenny and I started hanging out with him and his friend Steve but I was wary about letting things develop because Trev was black and I knew how my parents would be if they found out I was seeing him.

One Friday my parents were going out for the evening and I was babysitting. Jenny came over, but while we were sitting chatting about 'the boys' there was a knock at the door. It was Trev and Steve. I started to panic. If my parents came back, they would kill me.

I calmed down when they said they had only come to drop off a bottle of wine for us and would leave after a drink. They left, as promised, and even gave Jenny a lift home. I cleared up any evidence of other people in the house. The cans and cigarette ends were put in a black bag and tossed over the back fence; I sprayed air freshener so they couldn't smell men's deodorant. I was so paranoid.

I sat on the sofa and, suddenly, the room started to spin. I had a burning sensation running down my back. I got up, feeling really woozy, and started walking up the stairs to the bedroom. That's all I remember. I woke up in a hospital bed with Mother and Dad sitting next to me. I could tell by their faces that they were not happy about something. A doctor checked me over but when he left Dad spoke in a low, menacing voice.

'Fuck. You had boys in my house,' he said. 'Now you're ill 'cause you've been smoking wacky baccy with them. When you get out of hospital, you're out!'

He poked his bony fingers into my leg, his long nails leaving dents in my skin. I tried to tell my parents they were wrong, but the next-door neighbour had seen them leave.

'We weren't smoking anything but cigarettes,' I said, but he wouldn't believe me. I had collapsed due to a severe kidney infection and stayed in hospital for two weeks, but still they blamed it on having drug-taking boys in the house.

Aside from that first night, my parents didn't visit me much – an hour in the evening if I was lucky. They refused to bring Alan or Audrey in either. As far as they were concerned, I was dirty and had brought shame on the family.

When the doctors deemed me well enough to leave hospital, my parents picked me up. Back at the house, Mother packed my stuff into black bags – clothes, shoes, toothbrush. She'd even removed my bed from the room. My sister already had a new double bed. It was like I had never lived there.

That evening I rang Jenny, and her mum picked me up from Stockland Green. I stayed the night at her house and the following day I got in touch with Trev. He said I could stay at his mum's house for a couple of nights. He slept on the sofa, while I had his bed.

I called home, but Dad slammed the phone down on me. I turned up at the door, but it was slammed in my face. In a weird way, I could understand his rage. His house: his rules. I wasn't his problem. But Mother? How could she just stand there and watch someone kick out her own daughter? And not only that, but actively help to pack up all her things.

Eventually, if Dad wasn't there, Mother would speak to me. Dad had banned me from the house, so to speak to her I had to meet her on the high street or pop round when he was at work. For the first time we shared a secret that didn't involve him. I wanted to take Alan and Audrey to the fair. Mother was scared Dad would find out, but she said yes, as long as no one told him. She even got the siblings to lie about it. This was a first. Maybe she felt guilt after all.

Trev's sister let us stay with her for a while, so we slept on the pull-out sofa and watched videos all night. One day she said we could have her flat, as she was going to stay with her mum. We just had to pay for the electric and our food. It was a lovely little flat, cosy, but it wasn't home. I should've been on cloud nine. We had our own place, our own rules, but some days we struggled to eat and, as much as I liked living away from my parents' influence, I had never felt so lonely.

In time, Dad let me back in the house, but on one condition. He believed I was going through 'a stage', and he had a proposal for me. He wanted me to go to Slough to stay with friends. It was to help me clear my head.

By then, I had given up the college, but I continued to work at the residential home.

Telling Trev was the hardest thing I had to do. He and his family had shown me nothing but kindness, but I still craved my parents' attention. It was impossible for anyone to understand unless they had been in my shoes. Oddly, them sending me away had made me feel special. It made me feel like they actually cared about me. Trev begged, pleaded, cried, but I had to go. If I stayed, I would only hurt him even more.

The woman I stayed with in Slough was called Jill and she treated me like a young woman. I could eat when I wanted, sleep when I wanted, go where I wanted – within reason – and talk when I wanted. She even let me keep in touch with Trev. I could not understand why she was friends with my parents. She had a daughter called Tee, and many evenings we would put on our pyjamas, make hot chocolate and chat about everything.

After five weeks my parents came to get me. They said I looked so much better now I was away from the bad influences. Dad said I could come back home. As sad as I was, and knowing that I'd never see Trev again, I felt like I needed my family more, so I did.

Willingly, I went back to the family that had caused me so much misery.

As soon as I walked through the door, things went back to how they were before. I was back to being the babysitter, and my parents had even managed to set up new friends for me. Denise, who lived next door, was also mixed race, so I was a little shocked they allowed the friendship, but her mother was an old friend of my mother's family. I was so embarrassed when she came round; it was like a set-up, like I couldn't find my own friends.

It wasn't as bad as I feared, however, as Denise turned out to be someone with whom I had a lot in common.

Some nights she liked to have a spliff while I had a coffee with her mum.

One particular night, we were at her house and Denise was rolling one when some of her friends came round. We all sat around drinking beer. She offered me the joint and, without a second thought, I took it. I had never touched drugs before this, so when my throat went dry I panicked, thinking I was about to swallow my tongue.

After midnight, everyone went home, but I stayed and carried on drinking. All I remember was the loud bang on the front door. It sounded like the house was being invaded – the bang shook the walls and made Denise and me jump.

'Tell that little druggie she's not living in my fuckin' house any more.'

It was Dad. I jumped up, ran into the kitchen and washed my face in cold water, trying to wake myself up. When I came back into the living room, the house was silent. Denise was sitting there, shocked.

I counted the twenty-three steps back to my parents' house. I walked in and the house was in complete darkness. The hairs on the back of my neck stood up as I listened to my parents mumbling upstairs. Their bedroom door was closed, so I couldn't hear what they were saying. I went into the front room and sat on the chair in darkness, trying to straighten out my head, thinking where I could go now I'd been kicked out again. How did they know? Could they hear us? It wouldn't surprise me if they had a glass up against the wall. I started to cry. It was about two in the morning and I had to find somewhere to live.

I woke up in hospital.

This time, instead of my parents sitting next to me, there was a complete stranger. She was a counsellor and was asking me questions about the night before. I couldn't remember. Why was I in hospital?

I had taken an overdose of Dad's heart medication. I was lucky. Apparently, the pills, mixed with the level of alcohol in my system, could have killed me. I never uttered a word. I just lay there and cried.

The nurse came round and said I could go home but had to wait to be picked up. They had informed my parents. I just had to wait for them to come. They didn't.

Denise came to get me. I could hardly walk, but she helped me get dressed and walked me down to her car. I didn't have to ask where my parents were; the silence and their absence said enough. When we got back I went into Denise's for a coffee. I started pacing her living room, trying to get the feeling back in my legs. They felt like jelly and I found it really hard to walk, but I had to; I couldn't sit around and wait. After about an hour and still not feeling too good, I braced myself for the confrontation.

I knocked on the door and waited. I needed sleep. I wanted to go to bed and deal with things the following day. Mother opened the door and walked off.

Did I just go in? Was this a trap? I walked in gingerly,

closing the door as quietly as I could. My parents didn't speak to me. I sat in the lounge, staring out of the window, waiting for the showdown. There wasn't one.

After a while, my parents went to bed and I relaxed, thinking it was going to be OK. I went to bed hoping that the whole situation would blow over. More fool me. You'd think by now I would have known better.

I was woken the next day by the sound of bags being thrown on to the bed I was sharing with my sister. They were filled with my clothes. Mother dragged me out of bed.

'Get dressed and get out,' she said.

I didn't even have time for a wash. I stood outside with the few belongings I had. I ended up at my nan's, but on strict instructions that Mother didn't find out. It was ludicrous. Every time they came to visit I hid in my uncle's bedroom. He had a lock on his door so even when they tried to go snooping – which they did – they didn't find me.

One day I sneaked out and spoke to my sister, without them seeing. She seemed pleased to see me. I convinced her to give me her house key so I could retrieve the rest of my belongings. I nearly got away with it but, when I was returning to the house with my stereo and the other bits and pieces I'd had to leave behind, they saw me. Mother was all set to call the police before Audrey admitted she had given me the key.

I continued to stay at my nan's but, over the course

of the next few months, relations between my parents and me thawed. Gradually, they started speaking to me like a human being. I had forgotten what that felt like.

When I turned eighteen my parents took me out and I got really drunk. The following day, Dad said I could move back in with them. Something told me I was better off at my nan's, but that old craving for attention and respect returned and I went back again.

But things hadn't changed. My wages went to Dad and my spare time turned into babysitting again. I wanted to punch myself. What was wrong with me? The doctor said I was suffering with depression, but it felt deeper than that. Medication wasn't going to get me out of the cycle; I was sunk too deep in it.

I started working in a social club in the evenings – my parents' watering hole. They were there every weekend and often through the week, playing dominoes or snooker, but at least I didn't have that much to do with them, because I wasn't allowed to serve family and largely worked in the bingo room upstairs.

Next door to the bingo was the snooker room, where a barman called Graham worked. My friend had a thing for him, but at first I couldn't see the attraction. However, the more I got to know him, the more I found that he was cheeky and a bit of a charmer.

One night, after a family party at the club, I was waiting for a taxi when I heard Mother shouting over to me. She was talking to Graham and had this huge smile on her face.

'He's taking you out next week,' she said. And that was that. The next thing I knew, I had a new boyfriend and my parents were suddenly my best friends again.

Before our first date Graham was on the phone constantly, but I couldn't help wondering whether he was only going out with me because of pressure from Mother. I knew what she was like – pushy, like a dog with a bone.

On the night, Mother picked out what clothes I had to wear, even my shoes. She made me wear a short black dress with cream canvas boots. I should have been grateful for the attention – after all, this was what I had been craving – but I had never felt so uncomfortable in my whole life. When Graham turned up I felt uneasy, like a tramp.

I spent the night with Graham. I had never slept with a person on the first night, but I did with him. It may sound silly but, once we were alone, in the pub talking, I saw a completely different side to him and I could actually see myself with him, having a future together.

I fell for Graham hook, line and sinker and, after that first night, I knew we would be together for a long time. We lay in each other's arms all night, not wanting the morning to come. The only time I had felt that way before was with Mark.

However, when I got home, Mother was foaming at the mouth.

'You slut,' she said. 'Nothing but a slag.'

They tried to ground me, but that night I sneaked

out to see Graham. I saw him every night. After we had been pushed together, I fell for him – and hard. Graham took a whole week off work and I spent it with him. We got to know each other better, talking about past relationships and our childhoods. Graham was an only child so there was never any sibling rivalry for him. His parents had split up a few months prior to us getting together. His mother had run off with another man who was the same age as him, and Graham was quite volatile in his attitude towards her. He would call her all sorts of names and vowed never to forgive her for leaving his dad. I told him about my relationship with my parents. He didn't seem shocked. He knew Dad from the club so knew how overbearing he could be.

I had started working at a shoe shop on the high street. The job wasn't well paid, and most of my money went towards rent, even though I was hardly ever at home. As Christmas approached, I literally had no money to buy presents for anyone.

My parents were going on at me about it. I lied and said I had bought presents and that I had hidden them in my locker at work. Every evening when I went home I'd get asked about the presents, and again I would lie and say I'd forgotten them.

On Christmas Eve Graham picked me up after work. He offered to give me money to go shopping for presents but I lied to him too and said they were at home. We made plans to see each other on Christmas night.

When it came to exchanging presents on Christmas morning, my parents demanded their gifts.

'I've left them at work,' I protested.

'Bollocks,' Dad said.

I ran upstairs, but Mother chased me with the slipper. I dived on to my bed and tried to cover up as she rained the hard sole across my head. I screamed at her, tried to fight her back, but the beating seemed to go on for ever, my siblings watching from the bedroom doorway.

I ached, I was sore and my skin was burning. I lay in the foetal position on my bed and stared at the clock on the wall, wishing the hours away. Mother said I wasn't going anywhere, but I was determined I was getting out of the house one way or another.

Dad gave my presents – a mini stereo and some underwear – to my sister, who had already been showered with gifts of her own.

When Graham came to pick me up I sneaked out and stayed at his place that night, and every night to New Year's Eve.

As the year drew to a close, my parents, auntie, uncle, cousins, nan, family friends and I went to the club. There was entertainment on, and Graham was working so I went along just so I could spend time with him. I enjoyed myself and danced all night.

When we all headed back to Denise's house, though, the atmosphere changed. One of Denise's friends, who had a thing for me and didn't like the fact that I was with Graham, called me a slag. I asked him to repeat it and, when he did so, I slapped him across the face.

Mother suddenly grabbed me by my hair with one hand and punched me with the other. It was like everything was happening in slow motion. I could see everyone standing there, watching me getting my head kicked in by my mother. She dragged me to the floor, but I managed to grab the table and haul myself up.

More people waded into the fight but I broke free and ran next door to my parents' house. As my parents' friends tried to calm Mother down, Dad came running into the lounge and pulled me up by my top.

I tried to tell him it was Mother who had gone for me, but he didn't want to listen. In the middle of the lounge was a large round glass coffee table. He smashed his hand down and, as it shattered, I turned my back, but a large chunk of glass wedged into the back of my knee.

Blood started streaming from the wound, but even though I was screaming in pain no one called an ambulance. Dad just walked out.

A girl came to my aid and bandaged up the cut after pulling out the shard of glass. Graham then arrived with a taxi to get me out of there. As I walked out to the street, Dad grabbed my arm, trying to stop me.

Graham stood between us.

'Get your hands off her,' he said to my dad. 'She's coming with me.'

We got in the taxi and went to Graham's house. That night he asked me to marry him.

He'd saved me. Of course I said yes.

On New Year's Day 1996, I woke feeling like a completely new person. I was free again and, finally, I had found someone to love and protect me.

Graham had spoken to his dad, Terry, and confirmed that I was allowed to move in. The only thing I had to do was go back to my parents' house to get my stuff.

It was later that day when we pulled up outside. We looked at each other nervously. This wasn't going to be easy, but we were ready. I knocked on the door and waited. No answer. I knocked again. Still no response. I banged on the door and it flew open. Dad stood on the other side. He looked me up and down in disgust and walked off.

I didn't wait around. I flew up those stairs like I had rockets on my heels. Graham followed me and stood by the bedroom door as I randomly grabbed clothes and shoes and make-up. I filled carrier bags and old school bags – there was no way I was going downstairs to get a black bag. I shoved things in Graham's arms and put on about three coats. I was almost done when Mother appeared at the doorway. Luckily, Graham was in her way, but she never said a word. She just stood there, staring at me with those evil green eyes. I picked up my bags and squeezed past Graham and stood face to face with the woman who claimed to be my mother.

The coldness in her eyes made my blood feel foreign. I had no connection to this woman. I was about to start a new journey in my life and I didn't want her to be part of it. Recognizing that made me sad but the feeling only lasted a second.

Before my eyes could fill with tears I walked past her, down the stairs and out to the car, I filled the boot with my stuff and got in. I didn't once look back at the front door. I don't even know whether she watched us drive off. The relief was like a rush of adrenalin. I had never walked out before and, if it wasn't for Graham, I would have carried on just existing. I was looking forward to my future with a loving person in a beautiful house. My life was going to be perfect.

There was no way Mother was going to hurt me or have control over me again . . . or so I thought.

18

For several weeks Graham and I existed in our own little bubble at his dad's house. He took me to Stratford for the weekend. It was like living in another world. Never before had anyone been so attentive towards me.

Sadly, that early blissfulness wasn't to last. As we settled into a routine, arguments started to creep into our relationship. Little things would set us off. We were both strong-willed characters who were determined to stand our ground. Terry once complained about the shouting. I felt so ashamed.

So much for my brave new start. Within just a few weeks we were at my mother's, living in my old bedroom because things had become so strained with Terry.

We kept to ourselves but, not long after we moved back in, I started to feel ill. I was sick in the mornings, with dizziness and tiredness. We decided to go to the clinic to have a pregnancy test. A baby was something we both wanted. We'd been together for a year now, and had been trying for a while, but the doctor had said that because of my frequent kidney infections I might find it difficult to conceive.

Graham took the day off work and, first thing that morning, we went to town, to the clinic. I did the test and was told to go home and wait. I had to ring at a certain time with a reference number. We went home but didn't want to sit in the house. This was something we wanted to do together and on our own, so we parked the car and went to the club across the road. Graham sat with his pint of lager and I had an orange juice. I can't remember the conversation. We were talking babble, passing the time with small talk. We kept looking at our watches. The time came, and Graham gave me 50p for the phone. As I spoke to the receptionist my hands started to shake. I read out my reference number and waited for her to check. I asked her to repeat the results and asked if they could be wrong, but her answer was the same. I was pregnant.

Walking through the door, I didn't want to look up, but I had to. I had to look at Graham's face when I told him I was having his baby.

His face said it all. I feared for how Mother would react to the news, but Graham was happy and that was all I really cared about.

When I told Mother she hugged Graham and congratulated him. I got a 'well done'. Dad shook Graham's hand, while I got a tap on the shoulder.

Their attitude at the start surprised me. I thought they would have been hostile. However, as the weeks passed by, they reverted to type and tried every way possible to cause arguments between me and Graham. They took over my appointments, told Graham the baby would have my family name and that Mother would be there during the birth – none of which I agreed to.

I sat there thinking about Mother and what me having a baby would mean. I feared I would be a terrible mother, like she was. What if I lacked the same mothering instinct? Should I get rid of the baby? It was something I seriously considered for a while, but I couldn't do it. Despite my fears, I wanted this baby.

I believed Mother's anger stemmed from the fact that, with a family of my own, she'd no longer be able to control me.

One day when Graham finished his shift we went back to the house and sneaked in. The following morning we got up early and went out for the day. We didn't want to stay in the house, stuck in one room, waiting for my parents to kick off. I was even too scared to go to the toilet on my own, so Graham came with me.

We emerged to a barrage of abuse, but we ignored them and went back to the bedroom. When we came back from our day out, we pulled up outside the house and sat in the car for a while. We were too nervous to go inside.

Graham had a cigarette then we got out of the car to go into the house. As we got to the gate the front door opened. Mother came running towards us.

Graham stepped in her way and she bit him. Then she threw a punch that landed on the centre of my stomach. I went down. Graham helped me into the car and took me to hospital.

Luckily, our baby was fine and, after keeping me in for observation, the doctors allowed me home. The trouble was that – not for the first time – I was coming out of hospital with no home to go to.

Graham slept in the waiting room all night. We had a car full of stuff for a baby, but nowhere to go. We sat in the car for a while, just holding each other, while we came to the realization that we were about to become parents and yet we had nothing.

Graham drove down little lanes and through busy streets, just to kill time. We were preparing ourselves to sleep in the car when he got a call on his mobile from his nan. We could go and stay with her for a while. It could only be a temporary solution, though, so I went to the council and declared myself homeless. Within a week we were offered a two-bedroomed flat in Handsworth, an area of the city known as 'The Bronx'.

It wasn't the ideal place, but at least it was our own home, and it was exciting to get the keys. After we signed the papers for them we went back to Graham's nan's to collect our stuff and, on the way, a car hit the side of ours. We swung round, and our car went into some parked cars. We were both unhurt, but the car was a write-off. Not a happy start to our new life.

We moved in with our clothes, a rail to hang them on, the sofa bed from Graham's nan, a TV and a stereo. Our first meal was a tub of Super Noodles. We didn't care – it was our own place. All that mattered was that we were together and that our baby was OK.

When I was five months pregnant Graham's mum, Fran, treated us to a holiday in Cyprus, while Terry paid for new carpets for the living room and nursery. He also donated us his old furniture so, gradually, our flat became more like a home. The only thing I wanted for was company. Graham worked all day and went to snooker in the evening. I lived in an area where I knew no one. Every day I had to give myself a pep talk just to get to the shops.

As my due date drew nearer, I started to get more scared. The thought of giving birth terrified me. I really didn't like pain. Mother started ringing me a couple of times a week, asking how I was. She told me she missed me. I had rarely heard her say that before, but after our last altercation, when it seemed she was dead set on harming my baby, I didn't want to trust her. Slowly, however, she wore me down and I let her back in again.

Graham didn't want me in the flat on my own, so Mother said I could stay at their house. It was about the first time she had ever been nice to me. Graham dropped me off at my parents' every morning at half seven. My sister would be getting out of bed to get ready for school and I would jump in to catch up on sleep. Mother cooked my lunch, made me drinks and cooked tea for both Graham and me. She was behaving like a proper mother. Why couldn't she have been like this a little earlier, and more often?

At ten days past my due date the hospital said I should come in to be induced. It was March 1997, and

I was nineteen years old. Two days later, after gas and air, pethidine for the pain and an epidural, the doctors said I needed a Caesarean section. Mother attempted to take over, as usual, trying to push Graham out by saying that Dad would be going into the theatre with me. Luckily, Graham stood his ground and told the nurses to keep them away from me. On the way to theatre the pain had started again, and the doctors began to top up my epidural. My baby was in distress and, by the expression on Graham's face, things were not looking good.

As the doctor started to cut me, I felt the tear. I tried to scream out but a mask was placed over my face. I woke up in a huge pink room on a bed covered in blood and no one but a nurse for company. I was weak and tired and alone. I didn't know where my baby was and Graham was gone too.

I started to cry, then the door swung open and in walked Graham, holding our baby girl. He had been in the room next door feeding her and showing her off to his family. As he placed her in my arms the overwhelming feeling I got was unbearable. I cried with pride. She was perfect and she was mine.

Princess, as she was known for those first few moments, was born at 7.30 p.m. and visiting time was over by 8 p.m., so by the time we went back to our room, everyone had to go home. I had my own room and the nurse switched off the main light and put on the night-light.

I lay with my daughter in my arms and studied every

single detail of her face. I counted every finger and toe and kissed every part of her tiny head. I could have stayed in that room for ever. I felt safe, contented and, no matter how much pain I was in, elated. The nurses took my baby to the nursery for the night while I rested.

It was only later the nurses told me my heart had stopped three times while I was under the anaesthetic. Graham had been removed from the room while they resuscitated me.

I woke early the next morning feeling empty. I wanted my baby. I pressed the buzzer three times. I had to convince myself I wasn't dreaming, but when the nurse finally brought in my baby all my fears disappeared. I was a mummy, and I did have a beautiful daughter.

Nothing could knock me off that huge platform I was standing on. I whispered in her tiny ear, promising that her mummy and daddy would always love each other and her. I promised her the moon and stars, that she would never ever go without and that her life would be happy.

We called her Sianie-Louise and, from that first moment I held her, I knew I wasn't going to be like my mother. My daughter was not going to be made to feel like an outsider or live like a slave. Her life was not going to be as blighted as mine had been.

19

I so desperately wanted the happy glow I had from holding my newborn baby to last, but a combination of factors led to me becoming depressed. Firstly, the flat was cramped, and it wasn't ideal having Graham's mother living with us for a time after the birth.

In addition, Graham wasn't getting on with my parents. The kindness Mother had shown me in the lead-up to Sianie's birth was soon a distant memory.

Graham's cousin had a house in Kingstanding, an area nearby and to the west of Erdington, and, as she was moving out, we applied to the council to exchange with her. It was a proper little house, with two bedrooms and the tiniest bathroom, but it was a chance for us to make yet another fresh start, hopefully without our parents' interventions.

As we settled into our new home things started to fall into place. Graham stayed home more, and the arguments between us subsided. His cousin Sally lived in the same street with her family and she became one of my closest friends and someone in whom I could confide.

In the meantime, my parents were celebrating a huge payout from the council for the dilapidated state of our old house. The extra money meant their social life improved. They could afford holidays, and they even paid for a twenty-first birthday party for me – although footing the bill meant they controlled the guest list.

When Sianie was around eighteen months old I took her to playgroup every Wednesday morning. I sat on the side with a cup of orange juice and watched my baby running around with the other children, squealing in delight when she was being chased and giggling as she went down the slide.

One morning she was playing on the little red slide when, without warning, a small boy pushed her over the side. My heart stopped as I watched my baby's head hit the ground. I couldn't get to her quick enough. I scooped her up in my arms and started checking for bleeding and bumps. Not one person came over to see if she was OK. I shouted at the mother of the child who pushed her to keep her child in check. I grabbed the pushchair and stormed through the double glass doors, slamming them shut as I left.

When we got outside my head was spinning and I began to cry. This was my precious baby. I never wanted to see her get hurt. I wanted to wrap her in cotton wool. I got home and paced up and down, waiting for Graham to come home.

Then Dad came on the phone. Mother had been taken into hospital with chest pains and he was leaving to come and get me so we could go and see her. He pulled up outside, beeping his horn. I picked up Sianie and ran out to the waiting car, leaving a note for Graham that I was visiting Mother. I knew he'd be angry that I wasn't home, but what could I do? Dad had told me I was going to see Mother.

On the way to the hospital I told Dad about what had happened at the playgroup and that I was worried. I wondered whether I should get Sianie checked out at Accident and Emergency. Dad started swearing, accusing me of being selfish and not caring enough about Mother.

I couldn't believe it. Here I was trying to focus on the wellbeing of my daughter, but it didn't seem to matter what I did, my mother's life sapped all my emotional energy.

'She looks fine to me,' he said. 'Stop being over-dramatic.'

No sooner had he said it than Sianie was sick over me. Dad went crazy, shouting that I would have to clean his car. I didn't care. I knew where my priorities lay.

As we pulled into the car park I grabbed my daughter and ran towards A&E. She threw up again. The receptionist rushed us through the double doors to a waiting bed and, within seconds, two doctors and a nurse were surrounding her. I felt helpless, watching the doctors take her blood and the nurse comforting her as she continued to be sick.

Sianie had suffered concussion from the fall off the slide and the doctors wanted her to stay on a ward overnight so they could monitor her. I sat next to her and kissed her hand, tears falling on to the crisp white sheets of her bed. I prayed. I couldn't remember the last time I had prayed, but that night I didn't stop. All I kept thinking was that I was a bad mother. I was afraid Sianie would be taken away from me.

A nurse rang Graham and he joined me at her bedside. By this time, Dad had established Mother was going to be OK and had gone home. Graham and I stayed with our baby through the night. She was dehydrated from the vomiting, so the nurses told us to buy bottles of cola and let the fizz out. The flat drink would rehydrate her. Graham bought about six bottles and she drank almost the lot. She was allowed home the following day and we took her out and spoilt her rotten. She was so much better. It was as if my prayers had been answered.

In October 1998, when Sianie was nineteen months old, I discovered I was pregnant again. This time, not everyone was as happy as I was.

Graham's family said Sianie would end up going without because she wouldn't be an only child any more, while Mother bluntly told me to terminate the pregnancy and 'get rid of it'.

'You don't want to be saddled with another baby at your age,' she said, giving me a glimpse into the way she thought about children, perhaps.

My second pregnancy didn't go as well as my first. One sunny afternoon I was sitting on the doorstep reading a book when my face started to tingle. It was such a weird feeling. I remember *Home and Away* started and I tried to whistle the theme tune but nothing came out. I tried to drink my coffee, but my mouth wouldn't work. I ran into the living room and stared at my reflection in the mirror. One side of my face had drooped. I thought I was having a stroke.

Instead of calling someone, I grabbed my little princess and locked myself indoors. Graham came home, took one look at my swollen, droopy face and laughed.

'You look like the Elephant Man,' he said.

Only after he had had dinner did he take me to the hospital. I was diagnosed with Bell's Palsy, the name given to facial paralysis with no obvious cause, and prescribed steroids. I had to go to the hospital every week after that, as I could only take the steroids on alternate weeks. Every week I had a blood test and every two weeks a scan to make sure the baby was OK.

My baby girl Tamzin was born ten days late, at 5.30 a.m., delivered by another Caesarean section. I had my own room again on the ward so, as with Sianie, I took advantage of the peace and quiet and studied my new little angel in detail. Ten fingers and ten toes, and with bright red hair, she was lighter and smaller than our first child. She seemed so tiny, and no newborn clothes would fit her. She had to have clothes meant for premature babies.

When I came home I found the house in the same state as our old flat had been. I put it behind me, though, tidied the place up and carried on as before. It took a while for Graham and I to adjust to our new family unit. At first I feared he wasn't going to bond with his new daughter and it seemed we were drifting apart but, as the weeks went by, we grew closer again and he and Tamzin hit it off to such a degree she became a complete Daddy's girl.

As the children got older, I started having driving lessons. It was my freedom, my taste of independence – a chance to do something for me. Graham had started a new job as a bailiff and it allowed me to take three lessons a week. I studied hard for my theory and passed first time.

I so desperately wanted to create a stable family life for my two daughters but, increasingly, our circumstances seemed to make that impossible. Graham had problems at work and, when he wasn't working, he was playing snooker, so we hardly had any quality time together. I yearned to give my children the upbringing I never had, but the longer things went on, the more I feared I might not be able to deliver.

At the end of September 2001 Sally and her husband, John, organized a weekend away in Blackpool. My parents took the girls and it was going to be a make-or-break trip for Graham and me. We needed to talk about where our relationship was going, because we couldn't go on like this any longer. It always felt like there was constant pressure to be nice to each other; we had stopped talking and listening to each other months ago.

Pulling up outside the bed and breakfast, I felt

optimistic. Graham was lavishing attention on me, tending to my every need. Up in our room it was as if we had met each other for the first time all over again. We talked, we hugged, we made love. Things felt good and we both promised each other that we would work hard on our relationship. We agreed what we had was special and that our little family was too precious to split.

Graham even asked me to marry him again. Every month when he got paid Graham would always ask me to run away with him to Gretna Green and get married. I would always laugh it off. I didn't want to get married. Admittedly, I said yes that first night – we were caught in the moment, the romance of being alone – but I always knew his possessiveness wouldn't change. In the evening, we got up, got dressed and met the others on the promenade. As we walked through the crowds, the sound of fireworks popping in my ears, I felt in love again. It was like we had rediscovered each other and the thought of ever being with anyone else was far from my mind. I had children with this man, we had to build a future for them and we owed it to them to stay together. I didn't want my children having different daddies like in my family.

Back home, however, things slipped back to how they were before we went away. Graham was back on the night shifts and still went out on his nights off. We were like passing ships in the mornings.

I started working as a community health worker and was quickly promoted to supervisor. When I wasn't working, I was with my children. My hours were worked around them. That was the golden rule of me returning to work.

We tried to soldier on, but we were only delaying the inevitable. Something had to give and, for the sake of us both, I had to call time on our relationship. I'm sure, looking back, we both did things that hurt the other but, ultimately, I had to do what was best for my precious girls.

It had almost felt worthwhile, the abuse and the mental torture I suffered as a child, if it had led to me having my own family. Or that's how it had felt at first. When I split from Graham, though, it broke that feeling of security.

At twenty-four, I felt washed up – I was a single mother of two young children. My girls were everything to me. I devoted my life to looking after them. But, as Graham and I divided the childcare responsibilities between us, I found I had time on my own for the first time in five years. It was a recipe for disaster – and my life threatened to spiral out of control.

20

What I needed was a pick-me-up – a tonic to get me back on my feet. It came in the shape of Tony, an unfeasibly good-looking lad who moved into the neighbourhood. When Tony started showing an interest in me, I could scarcely believe it. He was a few years younger than me, tall with dark hair and brooding eyes. He always looked and smelled good and the fact that he wasn't put off by my status as a single mum was powerfully appealing.

Tony started to come over to my house more often once Graham left. Some of my friends had reservations about him. I was coming out of one long relationship. Why was I getting involved with someone else so soon? I told them he was being more supportive than anyone else. Since Graham had left I hadn't heard a thing from my parents, and none of his family called to make sure we were OK.

I was flat broke, with bills to pay and food to buy, and Tony helped me forget about my daily worries. We should never have got together, but I was in such a desperate place that, to me, then, he was perfect. I should've known better really, especially when, after only a week of us seeing each other, he showed what a very jealous person he was.

Tony hated the girls talking about Graham. He was still their dad and I was keen for them to see him as often as they could, but Tony forbade Graham's name being mentioned in the house.

My old boyfriend Mark came round for a drink and a chat but Tony didn't like that either. One night he flipped, suspecting me of flirting with him. I should have known then that Tony was bad news. I had no good reason to stay with him, but I couldn't help it. I was infatuated with him, but I couldn't tell Graham. I felt guilty, even though I had no reason to.

It was inevitable that Graham would find out about Tony, and it happened on Christmas Day. At 6 a.m. I was woken by the sound of someone knocking at my door. I looked out of the window, and there was Graham's car. He had come to see the girls open their presents. I didn't mind that – in fact, I had invited him. I had one problem, however. Tony was in my bed!

I had told Graham to come over at seven. The girls hadn't seen Tony in the mornings. I was always adamant that he left before they woke up. I didn't want them to know that he was staying over. He had nothing to do with my girls. They had a dad, and I didn't want to confuse them. I rang Graham on his mobile and told him to go home, to come back in an hour after I'd had a shower and the girls were up.

He drove round the block, giving Tony time to disappear and me to have a quick shower.

I let Graham get the girls up while I started breakfast. The Christmas CD was playing and the bacon was under the grill. The girls were squealing with delight at the sight of all their presents. Graham helped them rip off the paper and watched in excitement as our babies caused a commotion.

For a minute, I forgot about the past. Everything felt normal, right, undamaged. I smiled as I watched my broken family laugh together.

After the presents were opened I served up breakfast. The girls wanted boiled eggs and soldiers, while Graham wanted a bacon sandwich. I had my usual – coffee and a ciggie.

Just after I handed Graham the plate, I heard an almighty smash. The plate had been thrown to the floor, bacon sandwich and bits of crockery everywhere. I spun round, and Graham's face was red with anger.

'Goodbye,' he said.

He grabbed his car keys and left. He revved his engine and spun his tyres as he sped off down the grove. I had been careless. Sitting there on the side was a huge 'Girlfriend' Christmas card and, to top it off, Tony had written 'love' inside. That's why Graham flipped. Since that moment, he has accepted no responsibility for the breakdown of our relationship.

For a few weeks afterwards, Graham stopped seeing

the girls. He took his anger with me out on them. He ignored my texts and refused to see me.

On the other hand, Tony was into me but standoffish with my girls. His jealousy got to the point that he hated me spending time with my own children. When he was in a good mood, though, he was the best company ever. I felt privileged to be with someone like him.

His downfall, however, was drugs, prescription and recreational. He loved going to music festivals and raves and liked going to Amsterdam with his friends. I know most sensible women would reel back in horror at all that, but I couldn't help it – I was falling in love with him.

Over time I worked out an arrangement with Graham whereby he could see the girls again. He would drop them off on Sunday afternoons.

My life with Tony was completely different to how it had been with Graham. It was fast and frightening, very bumpy and volatile. With Graham, life had pretty much been on an even keel. We had a routine. Breakfast time, lunchtime and teatime were all regimented. Dinner would be cooked and on the table by five o'clock; the girls would be bathed and settled by seven. Washing and ironing was done on a Saturday, the whole house was cleaned on Sundays and every day in the week I dusted and vacuumed the house.

Tony didn't want his dinner at five o'clock. He wanted to eat at nine. We didn't take the girls anywhere together or go shopping together. I was living as a single parent but trying to give Tony as much of my time as possible.

I told myself I was having the time of my life, but I had a good reason to be scared of Tony. He was very quick with his hands but also extremely quick to switch on the waterworks to make you feel bad.

I remember one time, we had had a lovely evening. We went for some food, watched a film and decided to have an early night. We were writhing around on the bed, declaring our love for each other, when suddenly his hands were around my neck. I couldn't breathe. My heart was pounding. I could feel the blood rushing through my head. I grabbed his hand and tried to release his grip, but I literally had no energy, I had to let go and wait. Within seconds, he stopped.

As he lay on top of me he stared down and started stroking my face. I pushed him off but as I tried to get out of bed he grabbed my arm and pinned me down. I had to lie there and listen to him whimper on about how his head had just gone and he hadn't known what he was doing.

After what seemed like ages, he fell asleep. I crept downstairs and sat on the sofa in the dark. I cried and cried and cried, until my face was red and tear-stained.

Tony must have heard me and came running down, rubbing his eyes.

'What's wrong?' he said.

I was speechless. I just stared at him. Couldn't he see what he had done? He needed help, but telling him that didn't help the situation. In a moment he was gone, out the front door and back to his mum's house.

I couldn't go on like this. I was ending up like my own mother – never getting respect from the opposite sex yet not wanting to be on my own.

I knew I should have broken it off with Tony then, but something told me not to. I was sinking further into depression and any sense of self-respect I had was evaporating by the day.

On one occasion I was at my parents' house with the girls. Dad and my sister were at work and I was having a coffee, watching my girls play with their dolls. Mother was sitting with me when my brother burst through the door and started swearing at her. I told him to stop swearing in front of the girls, but he persisted. He was towering over Mother, booming instructions at her.

There was a time when I would have revelled in seeing Mother on the receiving end, but as I had recently felt that I was like her, I was starting to sympathize with her lot.

I stood up.

'Don't talk to her like that. Back off,' I said.

Alan left the room and I followed him. As he walked up the stairs I added: 'Show some respect.'

He turned and glared at me. He started walking towards me. I tried to walk off, but he grabbed me and pushed me backwards. I fell on to the tiled floor. Suddenly Mother was there, kicking me. She didn't care where – face, ribs, kidneys.

I managed to get her off by kicking out, catching her in the stomach. By then, though, I was covered in bruises.

I ran into the living room and grabbed my keys from the table. Sianie was screaming and Tamzin was hiding behind the chair. As I grabbed my youngest, Mother slapped Sianie around the face.

'You're better off without a mother,' she said.

I punched Mother in the back of the head and grabbed my babies, squeezing the life out of them as I ran, carrying them both in my arms. I jumped in the car and went to a friend's house. She only lived thirty seconds away. I was too shaky to drive any further.

My friend and her mum phoned the police for me, and they also called my dad. While I was waiting to give a statement I rang Tony, who was at work in a phone shop, but he couldn't speak because, he said, the store was busy.

I gave a statement to the police, but when it came to it I couldn't press charges. Even though she had attacked me – while I was defending her – she was still my mother. I couldn't do it.

The officers went to talk to her and told her to stay away from me or she would be arrested for breach of the peace.

I got in the car, head spinning and aching from having my hair pulled. I went straight to Graham's house and begged him to have the girls. I was a state. I was panicking over the girls. They shouldn't have seen that. It was all my fault. I had let them down. I left them there.

Back home, I sat in silence, replaying everything over and over in my mind. Tony called.

'I've spoken to your mum,' he said. 'She says you went to the house, picking on her son.'

I couldn't believe what I was hearing. I told him what she'd done to Sianie, but because he had never heard of a grandmother being so evil he said I was making it all up.

I put down the phone and collapsed. My head was spinning. I could still hear Sianie screaming – but she was with her dad. I could feel the kicks to my stomach and punches to my face – but I was alone. Over and over again, I heard Mother's voice.

'You're better off without a mother!'

I woke up to shining lights. I was dressed in a gown. I saw Sally. She was holding my hand and crying. I had taken an overdose. She had saved me. I had spoken to her beforehand apparently, and she had come to mine to make sure I was OK. She had banged on the door and because I didn't answer she booted it open and found me lying on my bed unconscious. As she called the ambulance, Mother had rung. There was no remorse.

When Sally told her how she had found me, Mother said: 'You'd better call the ambulance then, hadn't ya?'

I was sitting up in the bed when the nurse came to check my blood pressure. I asked if I could go home, but she said no. They were waiting for the mental-health team to come and see me. I had to get out. There was no way they were going to put me in the nut-house. I had to get to my girls. I managed to convince Sally to take me to the toilet so I could change from the backless gown into my clothes. From the toilet we rang a taxi and sneaked out of the hospital via the ambulance bay. In the taxi on the way home my head felt really light. My legs hardly worked and I was so tired.

The hospital rang my mobile, asking me where I was. A psychiatrist was waiting to see me. I told them I was going home, so the mental-health home team arranged to come and see me that evening.

I didn't speak to any of the family for quite some time after that. I deleted their numbers from my phone and blocked Mother from contacting me in any way. Things weren't the best, but they were better the less I dealt with them.

I learned to read Tony, look for the mood and take it from there. That became my motto every day. I had to keep the relationship with him apart from the one I had with my girls. He was jealous of the time I spent with them. He made no secret that he loved it when they went to Graham's. That's when I saw more of him.

His drug use continued. I couldn't control that. He smoked solids, took pills and cocaine. When we had the weekends to ourselves, Tony would be off his face and I had no idea what to do.

It makes me ashamed to admit it but I felt that, to get to Tony's level, I had to do the same as him. So – only when the girls were not at home – I joined him in taking cocaine and ecstasy. For a brief few hours I forgot my problems but, deep down, I knew I was only storing them away for later.

Tony's moodiness never changed, but I did. I started to lose all self-respect. On drugs, he became so loving, telling me I was the only girl he had ever loved. When he was coming down, however, he couldn't stand me. I became obsessed with him, even giving him the money to buy drugs. If I was out of cash, I didn't see him. It was a vicious cycle.

Amid it all, I became pregnant with Tony's baby but, without a second thought, I knew I had to abort it. I was already a single mum of two children, plus I knew the relationship was too destructive. I knew I wasn't going to be with this man for the rest of my life – unlike the way I'd once thought I would be with Graham. I knew I had to get rid of the baby.

I didn't ask Tony for his advice. He knew what I was doing, but he didn't say I had to do one thing or the other. For that, at least, I was grateful. On the day, he sent me a text from his mother's house, wishing me good luck. When it was over, I felt numb, but relieved. He went back to his prescription pills.

That wasn't the end of it. The neighbours made trouble with Graham's family, saying I was doing drugs with lots of different men and the girls were being neglected. They complained to the council that I was throwing parties and was guilty of antisocial behaviour. The council threatened me with eviction.

I could slowly feel myself going mad. It got to the point where I barely recognized myself. I was underweight and pale.

The situation with Tony was reaching boiling point and the night things came to a head I was watching a movie with him, an old friend called Stephanie and her boyfriend, David. When it finished they left and Tony decided to go to the off-licence for more beer. I had a shower and settled into my pyjamas. I was chilling on the sofa watching another movie when he returned. I didn't really pay much attention to Tony when he came in. I knew he had been to his mother's because he had been gone for half an hour and the shop was only two minutes away.

He walked past me into the kitchen. I could hear him opening drawers and cupboards, muttering under his breath. Without saying a word, he walked past me again and went upstairs. I lay on the sofa watching the film, not taking any notice. I thought he had gone up for a shower.

Then I heard banging. I ran up the stairs to see what was going on. My girls were sleeping and I wanted it to stay that way. I went into the bedroom and found Tony pulling clothes out of the wardrobe – clothes I had ironed that day.

'What are you doing?' I said.

'Leaving,' he said. 'I don't want to be with you any more.'

'So you wait until I do the ironing before you leave,'

I said. I don't know why I focused on that. It was so absurd I giggled.

He grabbed a shirt and shoved it in my face.

'Cut my fucking clothes then,' he said. 'Go on.'

He pushed the shirt so hard into my chest my head snapped back. The adrenalin kicked in. I grabbed the shirt from his grip and ran down the stairs. I could hear his footsteps behind me. As I headed to the kitchen I grabbed a pair of scissors. Just as I went to cut the shirt Tony grabbed my hand. He squeezed so tight the scissors dug into my hand, I shouted out in pain and he released me. I dropped the scissors and tried to push past him but as I ran he moved and pushed me to the ground.

Tony stood over me and pulled me across the room by my hair. He dragged me over to the fire and sat on my chest, then leant forward and spat in my face.

I tried to grab my phone, which was on the sofa, but Tony laughed at me. I couldn't breathe.

Tony calmly called his mum and asked her to come over. I thought I was going to die. I could feel my throat getting tighter and drier. It was a horrible and strange feeling. I did think about playing dead, just so he would get off me. My automatic reaction was to try and fight back.

Just then Tamzin ran down the stairs. When she saw what was going on she jumped on Tony's back, screaming at him to get off her mummy. I could hear Sianie on the stairs screaming. Then there was banging on the door. It must have been his mum.

She shouted through the letterbox for Sianie to open

the door but, God bless her, she wouldn't. Tony released his grip and tried to grab Tamzin. I pulled my knee up to his groin and made him fall. I shouted at Tamzin to run. She ran up to her sister.

I grabbed my phone and dialled 999. I shouted at the operator to get the police, but Tony managed to grab the phone out of my hand and told the operator I was going mad and was waving knives around. I screamed, hoping the operator could hear me. I thought he would know Tony was lying. He hung up and stood up. It was over, I thought.

He turned and shoved me in my side. His mum was still shouting through the letterbox. Eventually, he opened the door and left. I lay in a heap on the floor, pyjamas ripped. It was a scene my children should never have seen. I was so ashamed.

I called Stephanie, and she came straight away. She took pictures and helped me clear up. The police got involved and for a stressful few months it looked like it might be me who would be in court for assault. The case was later thrown out, however.

The following night, after I tucked the girls up in bed, I sat in the darkness, waiting for the sun to rise, wondering what the hell I had done so wrong.

Something had to crack. I was with Sally when I started to hear screaming in my ears, but no one had said anything. I shook uncontrollably and cried like a child. I had cried many times, but not like this. I felt broken, not in two, but into many pieces.

I was finished. Everything had been stripped from me and it felt like my soul was lying bare for all to see. I was so vulnerable and scared. I had gone into melt-down.

Sally and I went to see my psychiatrist. We had managed to get an urgent appointment. I took one look at the doctor and flew into a rage. To me, her sympathetic smile was mocking me. The questions she asked made it feel like I was on trial. I threw files on the floor and swore like a sailor. It was little shock that I was sectioned. I refused to go at first. Who was going to look after my girls? Graham was too busy with his new life. I hadn't spoken to my parents for months, but now, as I hit rock bottom, they were all I had. I needed them to help me. I had barely spoken to Mother since she had attacked me when I was trying to stick up for her against my brother, but here I was, begging her to look after my girls for me. They agreed – but only when I agreed to give them my family allowance.

After picking them up from school and nursery, I handed over a bag of clothes, along with my family allowance book, kissed my babies and went to the recovery house the doctor had recommended.

It was an old house, and very quiet. I was shown to my room; there was just a single bed and a chair. I folded my clothes and stacked them neatly on the floor. I then went downstairs to have a wander.

The lounge was full of books and paintings. It had a musty smell, but it all looked clean. The kitchen cupboards were allocated to the patients. My cupboard was empty, as I had handed over what money I had to my parents. As long as my girls were eating, I would get by on chewing gum and water.

No one told me what I could or couldn't do while I was in there, but the amount of drugs they gave me left me incapable of leaving my room. My only visitor over the first couple of days was Mark, but I got to call my girls each morning and evening. That kept me going.

I felt I was walking around in a trance while the doctors tried to find the right medication for me. I was supposed to stay there two weeks, but halfway through week one I called my girls as per usual, and got Mother.

'How long we got your kids for?' she asked. I refused medication that day and went to my parents' house to make sure everything was OK. The situation was far from ideal but my main concern was my girls so, when I returned to the recovery house, I made sure I followed all the rules, took the medication and took part in counselling sessions. The doctors were not happy that I was going home, but I needed to be with my children so I slapped on a smile and told everyone I was fine and on the mend. I was far from fine.

Despite the way things had ended with Tony, I was heartbroken our relationship was over. He had shown me the attention I never thought I would have after Graham and, as much as I hated to admit it, I was obsessed with him.

At weekends I handed the girls to Graham and went

to hang out with old friends from the Greenford, the housing estate where I'd grown up. I began taking cocaine again and spent Friday nights until Sunday getting off my head.

As far as I was concerned, I was no better than my mother. Everything I didn't want for my children was happening. I was bringing different men into their lives.

I didn't become addicted to cocaine. During the week, when I had the girls, I was completely different. I didn't touch the stuff. At the weekend, however, I was on a path of self-destruction. I'd stay over at Stephanie's house and drive home still under the influence, after having only two hours' sleep.

I didn't think I could sink any lower. I was wrong.

After one particularly heavy night we came back from a club to find our local pub was shut. It was after 3 a.m. We decided to have one more line of coke before going back to Stephanie's house.

I must have passed out, because the next thing I remember I was waking up in the doorway of the pub. A lad I'd known for years was with me.

'You're all right,' he said. 'Here, have another.'

I went out on to the pavement and snorted a line of white powder off the ground. It was after 5 a.m., so I had lost two hours. I knocked on Stephanie's door and asked for my car keys. She refused to give them to me. I stormed past her, grabbed the keys, got in my car and drove home. I then passed out again.

When I woke up several hours later I was mortified

about what I had done. Driving in the state I was, I could have killed myself or someone else. I had to sort myself out. If I didn't clean up my act, I might lose my children.

I was sitting outside my house on the kerb when a man I barely knew from the street came out and chatted to me.

'Listen,' he said, after I had talked a little about my woes. 'You have two lovely girls in that house who need you. Forget everybody else. You don't need to be worried about them.'

For someone who didn't really know me to tell me what I needed to hear was a further wake-up call. That was it. I stopped drinking, stopped taking drugs and started cleaning up my act.

Over the next few weeks I tried to keep my mind busy by cleaning obsessively. Every weekend, I was on my hands and knees scrubbing the carpets. I redecorated and tried so hard to ignore the little niggle inside me.

It became a turning point in my life. I built a wall around my girls and me. It was going to take someone very special to break through.

One of the friends I called upon for counsel during those hard times was Rachel, my old neighbour from the last house I had in Kingstanding. She had been a really good friend to me during the fall-out from my relationship with Tony. We kept each other on the right road. She had her share of problems, and she had a child the same age as Tamzin and we became close. She often stayed over at mine. Her mum worked in a bakery and she came round with cakes and doughnuts. We would put the kids to bed, cover our faces with mud-packs and pig out on cakes.

Amid the chaos of my life, Rachel kept me on an even keel. She loved having fun and, on the rare nights when we had childcare, we'd go out and enjoy a drink and a giggle. On Sundays, Rachel cooked us dinner; on Wednesdays, we went shopping with her mum; and when the kids were sleeping, we would pop open a bottle of wine and talk late into the night. Life wasn't perfect, but I was recovering. Sometimes, out of chaos, change can do you good and, in those days, I was indebted to her support.

One morning, I dropped the girls off at school and went down to Rachel's. We were getting ready to go shopping. As I walked into the living room, my heart flipped.

Scott, her brother, was sitting on the chair eating his breakfast. He was five years younger than me and worked as a window cleaner. From the first moment I set eyes on him something happened. I can't explain what was going on inside my head but I knew I wanted him. After everything I had been through, I just wanted a bit of fun. At the same time, however, I didn't want to get involved with someone new. I still bore the scars from my time with Tony, and the last thing I needed was another relationship of any kind, not least with the brother of a really good friend.

I exercised some self-control – but that didn't stop me having some mischief.

It came to Scott's birthday and one of his presents was a new mobile phone. Cheekily, I offered to set it up for him and sneaked my phone number into his contacts. I was determined to get to know him better, and for weeks we texted each other, flirting and being suggestive. It was innocent fun, but a welcome distraction to everything else that was going on.

Several times Scott said he was coming to see me, but when the time came he backed out. It got to the point when I started to feel a bit stupid, chasing someone who obviously didn't want to be with me. I only went to Rachel's the times I knew he was at work. I didn't want to feel any additional awkwardness. The age gap was clearly a factor, I told myself, and he enjoyed hanging out with his mates. I was his sister's mate and a single mum to two kids.

Despite all the obstacles in our way, I decided to force the issue. I went over to his house and asked him out. I think he was surprised that I was being so forward but he didn't complain. We sat and chatted and, from the off, I found him easy to talk to.

There was a spark between us and we hit it off immediately, but something inside me reacted differently than in the other relationships I had been in. I don't know if it was a self-defence mechanism – if I was testing him – but once I'd got what I wanted with Scott I started to treat him terribly.

I sparked fights for no reason, even attacked him on occasion. It might be that I now expected men to be cruel to me so I wanted to get my retaliation in first, but Scott was different. He refused to rise to me. He didn't storm out in a rage like other men. He calmly waited until my tantrum subsided and picked things up where we had left off.

He was a natural with the girls and, unlike Tony, accepted us as a package. I wasn't ready to throw myself into another relationship but quickly I realized Scott was different from other men.

Not long after I got to know Scott, however, something happened that shook the very foundations of my already fragile life. The fall-out from my relationship with Tony – and the resulting police scrutiny – had led to ongoing grievances with some of my neighbours. I was beginning to think it might be best if I moved the girls from the house and started afresh somewhere else, but nothing could have prepared me for what happened next.

I was in the house one night. The girls were sleeping. Without warning, there was an almighty smash. Someone had thrown a brick through my front window. I was utterly terrified. Who would do that to a woman living on her own? I had my suspicions.

I couldn't stay in a street where my children's safety was at risk, so I went to see my local MP and councillor to ask about a move to a different council house. Their advice was startling. The only way for me to be moved to a different house was to make myself homeless.

I couldn't believe it. What could I do? I was

genuinely afraid that the window-smashing attack was a warning. If I didn't heed it, what would happen next?

Where could I go? Who would take a single mother and her two children at such short notice? As much as I hated the prospect, I only had one option.

I declared myself homeless and notified the council I was moving out of the house. I packed whatever belongings I could into the car, gathered my precious children and, with a heavy heart, headed to the last place on earth I wanted to be.

21

'Here she is . . . crawling back home again,' Mother said, a satisfied leer on her face, when I returned home.

In an instant I was a child again. She had a knack of reducing me to nothing.

Me moving back was confirmation of everything she'd ever thought about me – that I wasn't equipped to look after myself. I hated myself for going back. I should have cut all ties years before but it seemed every time I tried to make a new start something happened to send me back there. They knew they had one over on me. They were my last resort, and they knew it. It played into their hands perfectly.

If I wanted a roof over the girls' heads I had to fit back into my parents' schedule. That meant taking them shopping, making meals, being their dogsbody all over again. It was as if the previous ten years, from when I was aged sixteen to now, meant nothing.

The only difference this time was that, because I had children of my own, I was used to cooking dinner for other people and I would have been making it for the kids anyway, so I didn't mind that aspect so much.

The house was a bit cramped, but I moved into a room with a double bed, which I shared with the girls.

For a few weeks, it seemed tolerable. The girls appeared settled enough and Mother was behaving herself. She doted on Sianie, absolutely adored her. It was funny seeing her being so affectionate, but it reminded me of how she was with my sister. Mother was colder towards Tamzin, but I put that down to the times we had spent not speaking and figured she just needed time to build up a relationship.

Although living back with my parents was by no means a permanent solution, the set-up allowed me to get into a routine and make plans of my own.

I started doing community care work with the elderly, taking care of their needs in their own homes. I was contracted to a set number of hours, but often worked more. I made morning calls starting at nine o'clock, finished at two in the afternoon then started back out again about five in the evening, to finish at ten. The work was hard, but rewarding. It gave me a sense of purpose after so long existing on my wits.

I had only been working for about a week before Mother started.

One night I came back and found Sianie upset. When I asked her what the matter was she replied, 'It's Nanny.'

'What's she doing?' I said, my mind spinning with the possibilities.

Through her tears, my daughter said Mother was being mean to her little sister. I asked her to elaborate and she revealed that Mother was giving her food but not Tamzin.

Not only that, but Mother was giving Sianie treats and making Tamzin watch her big sister eat them in front of her. It was mental torture.

It was sick. I was horrified. I had no reason to doubt Sianie's word. She was the golden child in my mother's eyes – she had no reason to lie. Plus, I'd seen for myself Mother's differing attitude to her grandchildren. Whereas Sianie was always a slim girl, Tamzin was physically stronger. Mother teased her, called her 'fat' and had made quips that she needed to go on a diet. All this to a six-year-old girl?

I couldn't understand where Mother's treatment of Tamzin was coming from. In many ways, they were very similar. Tamzin looks like my mother. She has her colouring – blonde hair and fair skin – and shared elements of her personality. She is headstrong and, even from a young age, didn't mince her words. Tamzin wasn't afraid to tell you how it was and she would put my mother in her place. It was quite funny watching a young child speak her mind – but Mother didn't like it.

I was in an impossible situation. I couldn't do or say anything, because I had nowhere else to live and no other childcare. Ideally, I wanted them out of that house, but where would we go? If I made them homeless again, Graham might try to have them taken off me. I was never going to allow that. I didn't want to give him any excuse to cause trouble.

I can't explain how horrible it feels when you can't trust the person looking after your children. Some days

I tried taking the girls with me when I went out in the evenings. They fell asleep in the car while I finished my shift. It wasn't the existence I had planned for them.

Over the next few nights I left them once again in the house and hoped my mother would change her attitude to Tamzin. It was a forlorn hope.

I came home one night and found Sianie upset again. 'What's the matter?' I asked her.

'Nanny was really horrible to Tamzin,' she said. 'She got a knife and said she was going to stab her.'

I couldn't believe what was coming out of my daughter's mouth – the mouth of an eight-year-old girl. She said Mother had lost the plot with Tamzin and brandished a knife at her. My blood ran cold. Memories of that night when I was in my nightdress and she came for me with the knife flooded my mind. It was history repeating itself.

I told Sianie I was going to have it out with Mother.

'Please don't,' she said. She was shaking with fear. It was terrifying that their granny could have such an effect on them.

That was it.

Tamzin was tucked up in bed but I got them both up and, without getting them changed out of their pyjamas, carried them down to the car. There was no point in confronting Mother. Aside from Sianie's fears, I knew she would either deny it or lash out in defiance. I rang a friend, Becky. She agreed to take us in and gave us a bed for the night. It was a short-term fix, but we made do for a few nights. The only problem was that, if her partner stayed over, there wasn't enough room for me, so I had to sleep in the car. In the cold, cramped motor, I curled up and wondered how my life had turned out so messed up that we were in this predicament.

With all that was going on, I sat down with Scott and told him my life was too chaotic for us to continue seeing each other.

'I don't know where my life is going,' I said. 'It's not fair for you to hang around while I get myself sorted.'

He was upset. I'm sure he would have tolerated anything to be with me. He cared that much, but I needed to focus. My priority was my children. Until I had resolved our homeless situation, I couldn't handle anything else.

In the weeks after I left home, Mother didn't once ask me why I'd moved out in the middle of the night. I don't think she cared. As far as I was concerned, Mother had used up all her chances. No matter what happened, I vowed that as long as I lived I would never go crawling back to her door again.

We were nomads – living off the kindness of friends. It broke my heart to put the girls through it, but they never missed a day of school and, to anyone who didn't know, they looked as happy and contented as any other children.

My house in Kingstanding continued to lie unoccupied. I was still paying rent but I refused to take the girls back there while a volatile atmosphere existed with people in my neighbourhood. Graham took them at weekends to stay with him. I was grateful a relationship still existed between the daughters and their biological father but I felt guilty that I couldn't provide a stable home life for my children. Everything was my fault. Every decision I made was wrong.

Through a friend of a friend I rented a room for us in a house owned by a couple with a daughter who was older than my girls. It was the tiniest box room, yet the three of us squeezed in. Sadly, the couple weren't the nicest people. They smoked like chimneys so, when the girls went to Graham's at the weekend, they reeked of fag fumes. That was another thing for him to have a go over.

I tried repeatedly to resolve my housing situation but the council dragged their feet. They claimed that, because I had made myself homeless on purpose, it was my own fault. I pointed out I had only followed advice from my MP, but it fell on deaf ears. I had no choice but to continue living in a rented room.

As 2005 drew to a close, I thought if we could just have some permanence in our lives maybe we could turn a corner and make a new start in the coming new year.

I was on at the council constantly about a house but we were still effectively homeless. During these months I often thought about Scott and how things might have worked out differently between us if I hadn't had so much else going on.

Around Christmas 2005 my half-brother Alan told me that Audrey had been in touch with Scott. Her contact gave me an excuse to get in touch with him. I called him up on New Year's Day 2006. Incredibly, after the way I had treated him and what I had put him through, he still wanted to be with me. We met up but took things slowly. Neither of us wanted to get hurt again.

However, the New Year did seem to herald a new start. Within weeks – albeit after pressure from my MP and even the local newspaper – the council told me they had finally found us a home. They had a family waiting for my house in Kingstanding. It was perfect. I could move out of mine and they could move in straight away.

It was a two-bedroom house in Erdington. It wasn't as nice as the home I was leaving, but it was mine and it was a roof over my children's heads.

The majority of our belongings remained in the house in the grove, so Dad helped me move what we could load into a van. After we'd ferried everything to my new house, he gave me a warning.

'You've been given a new life, Collette,' he said to me, but the way he spoke was almost threatening. 'It's just you and the girls. Keep your head down. Don't get involved with men. Don't get involved with the neighbours.'

He was pointing his finger in my face. I was too scared to say anything so I kept quiet. I wasn't brave enough to tell him Scott and I were back together. I feared he would think Scott was wrapped up in the trouble I'd had in my old place. Plus, I wanted our relationship to flourish, and the only way it was going to do that was away from the prying eyes of my parents.

Two weeks after I moved in, my parents celebrated a wedding anniversary. They were on at me to join them for drinks in the local pub.

'I'll give it a miss,' I said. 'I've still got boxes to unpack and things to sort out. I just want a quiet night.'

Scott rang me and asked if he could come over. I told him the same as I'd told my parents, but he was happy to come over anyway. I still hadn't told my parents we were together. We were taking things slowly and were keeping it quiet. Audrey knew because she'd been in touch with him before, but we'd told no one else. We were sitting, just chatting, when Dad pulled up outside. I panicked.

'Quick,' I said to Scott. 'It's my stepdad. You need to hide. Get outside.'

Scott was furious, but he ran outside and hid behind a washing machine I was throwing out that was sitting by the side of the house.

Dad came in and started stalking the place, clearly looking for something, or someone.

'What are you doing here?' I said.

'I'm here to see who's here,' he said.

'No one's here,' I said, my heart in my mouth. I was scared. If Dad saw Scott, there was no telling what he would do.

He stayed for a coffee and a cigarette before finally he left to rejoin my mother in the pub.

Scott wasn't happy when he came back in. He couldn't understand why a grown woman would act this way in her own house.

I couldn't even explain it to him.

That episode made me realize, however, that we couldn't go on like this.

I found out Audrey had told Dad about Scott and that's why he came up. A few days later I plucked up the courage, sat Mother and Dad down and told them what was going on.

Dad shook his head. 'You know what's going to come of that,' he said.

He might not have liked it, but it cleared the air and allowed Scott to move in, which he did about a month later.

It was bliss. We were a proper little family unit. The girls were happy we had a real house again and they liked having Scott around.

The only drawback of having a fixed abode was that Mother knew where to find me. I had succeeded in keeping her at arm's length, but now I was in my own place she was all over me like a rash.

I had a habit of leaving my doors unlocked and she would wander in unannounced and demand cups of tea and snacks.

Sometimes I'd be in the shower when she would let

herself in and I'd hear her shouting: 'Collette, where are you?'

Even if she found I wasn't in, it wouldn't stop her ringing me on my mobile.

'Where are you?' she'd ask.

'Up the high street, shopping,' I'd say. 'Why?'

'Me and your dad are at yours. You'd better get back here because we're waiting outside and we want a coffee.'

Any normal person would have told them to come back another time, but my old conditioning kicked in and I dropped everything to run home to them. I realize now what a fool I was, but then, crazy as it sounds, I was still seeking their approval.

They treated the house like their own – and by that I mean they expected to be waited on hand and foot. It wasn't just me they barked orders at. Dad, in particular, was horrible to Scott.

I don't know whether he genuinely associated him with the trouble in Kingstanding or if he just didn't like the idea of another man looking after me, but he did everything he could to put Scott down.

If they were sitting around in the house, he'd demand Scott go into the kitchen and fix them a drink.

If the girls misbehaved and Scott told them off – as he was perfectly entitled to – Dad would say: 'Hold on a minute. You're not their dad.'

It stunned me that my stepdad could be so hypocritical, given how he treated me for years after he and Mother got together.

Scott would shoot me a look. The tension from their constant interference led to so many arguments between us.

Mother warmed to Scott, but she embarrassed us in different ways, like recalling the 'hilarious' times we had when I was growing up.

'Hey, Scott, has Collette told you about when I poured a bottle of ketchup over her head?'

Scott walked out of the room.

'What's the matter with him?' Mother said.

'He doesn't want to hear things like that,' I said. 'I haven't told him things like that.'

'It was funny at the time,' she said, laughing.

No it wasn't, I thought. Not then. Not now.

Although we had our rows, I was lucky that Scott valued what we had together above their constant interference.

Nothing was going to split us – least of all them.

We were in love and, when I fell pregnant a few months into our relationship, we were both ecstatic. I had none of the doubts that I had had with Tony. I knew I wanted to keep Scott's baby.

We were both devastated then, when I lost the baby after just six weeks.

In total, I lost three pregnancies with Scott. In each, I miscarried within the first two months. We were heartbroken. It seemed we were cursed. After the times when I had been with Graham and hadn't wanted any more children, I was now desperate to give Scott a child of his own.

Another person who was heartbroken for us was Wendy. She had grown so attached to the girls and was desperate for us to add to our family. Sadly, she now suffered from poor health after an operation had left her with nerve damage and in a wheelchair. Later that year she suffered a massive heart attack and died. We were all shocked and distraught.

Wendy had been the only person in my younger days who told me the truth. In many ways, she was the mum I never had, and she doted on my girls. I tried to give her the best send-off possible by organizing her funeral, arranging for a beautiful singer and a party afterwards at our house. She would be sorely missed.

Wendy would have been delighted when I fell pregnant for a fourth time in early 2007. Yet, given our recent track record, Scott and I feared the worst. We got past the crucial twelve-week stage but still I was worried that something could go wrong.

One morning Scott was working, and texted me: 'Be my wife for life. Marry me.'

I thought he was having a laugh. I mean, who proposes by text?

'OK then,' I texted back, thinking no more of it.

The next day he took me into Sutton Coldfield and into a jeweller's.

'Choose a ring,' he said.

I still thought he was joking, but I chose one and he bought it. That night we had a meal and Scott went down one knee.

'Will you marry me, Collette?'

I was so excited. 'Yes, yes,' I said.

Immediately, I said: 'Let's fix a date.' For him to ask me to marry him after all he had put up with was amazing. He had put up with so much crap, yet not once had he left me, not once had he thrown in the towel. Marrying him was the least I could do.

Every time we passed a little church on the way to Sutton Coldfield I thought if I ever got married that was where I'd want to do it. We enquired and booked a date for August 2007, when I would, hopefully, be six months pregnant.

Sally was going to be my maid of honour, and she, along with Rachel and Scott's mother, helped me with the preparations. Sally accompanied me to the National Exhibition Centre wedding fair and helped me with the food and all the arrangements.

A week before the wedding, Mother said to me: 'Col, your dad's got to walk you down the aisle.'

Dad was the last person I wanted to give me away. I might have had to call him 'Dad' since he married my mother but I didn't even want him at the wedding, let alone for him to be involved.

'No, he doesn't,' I said. 'I've already got someone to walk me down the aisle.'

It had been a source of sadness for me that I didn't have a father to give me away. I didn't want Phil to be involved either. Since that day when he'd shown up at the house, I'd seen him from time to time. As I got older, he and Mother would continue to see each other in the pub. It was like they still couldn't stay away from each other. Eventually, though, they started involving me in their game of deception and, crazy as this sounds, I started feeling sorry for Dad. I tried to remind Mother she was married, but she didn't care. Her antics finally put paid to my relationship with Phil.

No, when it came to who would walk me down the aisle there was never any doubt in my mind. My cousin Steven had been there for me throughout my life. He knew all about the beatings I had suffered and the misery I'd endured. Over the years he had been more than a cousin, more a best friend.

I thought, by telling Mother that I didn't want Dad involved, neither would attend the wedding. That was their style.

But on the day of the wedding I turned up at the church and there was Mother, standing outside the doors, clutching two ridiculous horseshoes and crying her eyes out.

'What are you doing?' I said, fearing some other stunt. Surely she wasn't going to ruin my one day of happiness? 'What's the matter with you?'

'Oh,' she said, still sobbing. 'My baby's getting married.'

I couldn't believe it. After all these years, suddenly I was her 'baby'. I ushered her inside and told her to sit down by Dad.

Determined not to let her spoil my big day, I smiled and, with my cousin by my side, I walked down the aisle. I saw my stepdad sitting there and felt no emotion, other than my happiness that I was marrying my Scott.

Throughout the ceremony I could hear Mother and Dad chatting loudly, like they were having a drink in a club. They had absolutely no respect.

After the ceremony, my parents' presence was putting a lot of people on edge, because everyone knew that once they had a drink in them they were likely to cause a lot of arguments.

We were having our photographs taken outside when Mother came up to me.

'Right, we're going now,' she said.

Secretly, I was delighted. They were going. But another part of me was thinking, Where are you going? This is my wedding day.

I then discovered that one of Mother's friends was also getting married that day and she was having a free bar. So they came to my wedding ceremony and then went to the friend's reception.

When we got to our reception, I grabbed the microphone.

'Just to let you all know, Maureen and Dave won't be here. They're going to a free bar somewhere else.'

Some people cheered. Their absence delighted everyone, not least of all me.

It was a lovely feeling to be married, to belong to someone, to feel part of a loving relationship.

We didn't have much of a honeymoon period, however. I was experiencing a difficult pregnancy. I was up and down, and I could have lost the baby several times. On one occasion, she was lying in a certain position and I was in agony. I went to the hospital. The nurse said if the baby had moved again in a particular way it could have snapped something in my back, leaving me in a wheelchair. It was scary.

When our baby was finally born in November 2007, she was a little miracle. We called her Tegan-Riley, with a middle name of Wendy, after my aunt. She had beaten the odds, beaten the curse that had plagued us since we got together. It was wonderful watching Scott doting over his new daughter, but he made sure he did not neglect Sianie and Tamzin. Unlike Dad, he showered them all with love.

It seemed we had weathered the storm, and started a new chapter in our lives – but it was one that was going to turn my world upside down.

22

I watched the fat tears roll down her cheeks and I thought, My God, you're actually human.

Mother was weeping. In all the years I'd tolerated her abuse I don't think I'd ever seen her cry – not real tears from the heart.

Yet here she was, bawling her eyes out. And it was all because I had told her that Phil, the man who looked on me as his daughter, had died.

He had suffered a heart attack on Boxing Day in 2008. I hadn't spoken to him since I'd cut him out of my life in my early twenties.

Now, as I was breaking the news to Mother, it was clear that still, after all those years, her feelings for him ran deep, even though this was a man who had beaten her black and blue on occasion.

'Where's the funeral?' she asked me repeatedly. 'Tell me. I want to go.'

I found out, but I decided I wouldn't go. I was scared how my stepdad would react if he found out. After the funeral had been and gone, she scolded me. 'You should have told me where it was so I could have gone,' she said.

'Dave is your husband,' I said.

'I just wanted to say goodbye,' she said.

When I took my first overdose, aged eighteen, I became a patient under the Mental Health Act. That meant I was referred to a community psychiatric nurse (CPN). I had regular meetings but, after a while, the CPN would leave and I would be assigned another. I had to go over the same story with the new one, so, over the years, we kept going over the same thing time and again. Rather than help me deal with my frustrations, these sessions succeeded only in making me angrier. I kept saying to each CPN: 'I'm trying to lock these memories away but you keep making me relive them rather than deal with them.'

The nurses prescribed tablets to help my moods but as time went by I was less than careful about taking them.

As the years went on, my faith in the health system dwindled. Increasingly, it felt as though I was on my own. Scott was brilliant. He was wonderful with the girls, but it was external influences that were putting pressure on our relationship.

In September 2010 my CPN asked if I wanted to see a psychologist. I reluctantly made the appointment, because I didn't want to talk to him if, like the other specialists I'd seen over the years, he moved on after a couple of sessions. I went along to the appointment, but I was really off with him.

'What do you want to know?' I said, rather grumpily. His name was James.

However, as we got talking, I felt able to open up to him and, as the sessions continued, I realized he was going to be there every week.

Gradually, James started knocking down the wall I'd built up around me. I don't know how he did it. When I finally opened up I couldn't wait to see him again. Even though I'd get upset during our sessions it was a release having him there listening to me. He was interested in what I had to say.

Although Scott knew about certain aspects of my background, I had never spoken to him about all the miserable things I had endured. I didn't want to hurt him. I wanted him to love me because of how I was, not because he felt sorry for me. Deep down, although I loved him greatly, I always thought he'd leave, just like Graham. But these sessions enabled me to involve Scott in my problems. He came to some of them and, with my psychologist's help, he learned how to handle me when I had my darker moments. And there were plenty of those.

Opening up about my past meant awakening some demons. Sometimes when I came home I got so scared I locked the doors, locked the windows, drew the curtains, shut myself in my walk-in cupboard and sat there trembling, convinced someone was going to break in and attack us.

Scott learned to hold my hand, talk me round and slowly help to draw me out of my black moods. It was going to be a long process.

In the lead-up to Christmas that year relations were

strained between Mother and Dad. He had long since stopped working, due to poor health, he claimed, while she was working full time as a carer. Mother confided in Scott that she was unhappy at home. She felt Dave was frittering away her money and was controlling how she lived her life, in the way they had done with me.

Other things were going on too, with Alan and Audrey, who continued to live at home, even with their respective partners, which led her to think she might be better off without Dave. It got to the point that I felt sorry for her. 'You should leave him,' I said, when I heard the extent of what she was dealing with. 'Just leave him.'

Audrey was expecting a baby with her boyfriend around Christmastime but, after New Year, Alan and his girlfriend planned to move into their own place. Mother was seriously considering joining them. Despite all the years when she'd sat back and done nothing to support me in that house, it gave me no pleasure or satisfaction to see her suffering now. I was pleased she seemed to be doing something about it.

On 18 December Mother rang me and asked if I would take her to the hospital for an appointment. She'd been suffering from headaches for a while and had had some scans. It seemed a routine appointment, but no one else would take her.

I sat with her when the doctor said he had the results of her scans. The cause of the headaches was a brain tumour.

Oh my God, I thought. I couldn't believe it. The doctor went on to say the tumour was operable and he felt confident she'd make a recovery, but Mother was in bits. I was shocked, but strangely numb. Here was someone I thought was going to be around for ever and for a doctor to say that I thought, Wow, something's got her. She's mortal after all.

In the car park Mother was weeping like a little girl.

'Come on,' I said, putting my arm around her. 'Let's get you in the car and get you home.'

Dad was very calm when we broke the news to him.

'OK, then, let's see what needs to be done,' he said. 'You'll be all right, babe.'

Mother had to go into hospital two days later for the operation, which was scheduled for Christmas Eve. Now they'd found the tumour there was to be no delay in removing it.

Meanwhile, Audrey was having serious complications with her pregnancy. She went into a different hospital and, although she safely delivered the baby, also, bizarrely, on Christmas Eve, she was put into an induced coma. She was suffering from cardiomyopathy, a heart disease, and at one stage it was uncertain if she would pull through. Her new baby girl was in a special care unit.

It was a highly stressful time for everyone and we were constantly shuttling between the two hospitals, which were nine miles apart.

Mother's operation was a success and by Christmas Day she was sitting up in bed, albeit very groggy and weak.

We held an impromptu Christmas Day at her

hospital bedside with Scott and the girls, where we opened the presents and tried to make do as best we could.

Over at Audrey's hospital, she was out of the coma and was doing a lot better. She'd be able to come home in a few days. Amid all the commotion, I felt no one was paying any attention to her newborn baby, which was still in the special care unit. It is horrible to admit it but, amongst all the stress and anxiety, all I could think was that these people had ruined Christmas for my children.

I tried to suppress those feelings, however, and the day before Audrey and the baby came home, Scott and I went to their house and scrubbed it from top to bottom. We sterilized the place and tried to make it as hygienic as possible for them all, given they were recovering from major illnesses and what they had been through.

When Dad and Alan walked in they took one look at us and said, 'What are you doing that for?'

I can't do this any more, I thought.

Audrey was discharged a day before Mother. As soon as she got home in the morning she rang me.

'You need to come up and look after the baby,' she said. 'I need to see Mum.'

I thought, given she had just come out of hospital, she would need some bonding time with the baby, but no. I was to go there that afternoon so she could see Mother, who would be home in any case the following day.

Wearily, I said OK, but before I went I had an appointment with James. We hadn't had a session for four weeks due to the Christmas break. There was a lot to fill him in on. When I had finished I broke down in tears.

'This can't go on,' he said. 'Every time we meet you are getting worse, not better. They are going to break you, unless you do something about it.'

'What do you mean?' I asked.

'I can't tell you what you should or shouldn't do,' James said, 'but unless you stand up to them or tell them they are no longer part of your life you are not going to get better.'

That afternoon when I got home I sat having a cup of coffee with Scott. The phone rang. It was Audrey.

'So, when are you coming down?'

Without even knowing I was going to, I said, 'I'm not.'

'What do you mean?' she said.

'I'm not coming down again,' I said. I didn't know where this was coming from, but now I was saying it I didn't want to take it back. 'I'm never coming down again,' I went on. 'I don't want you to bother me again. I want you to leave me alone. Stay out of my life. You've done enough damage.' And I put the phone down.

The look on Scott's face was a picture. He never believed I'd say anything like that to them.

Later, my mother sent me a text: 'Have you fallen out with me?'

'No,' I replied. 'I haven't fallen out with you.'

That was it. That was the last I heard from them.

When I could digest what had just happened I realized something had clicked with what James had said. It was like a light had been switched on. Unless I did something drastic I would always be running around after those people.

Another thing James said resonated with me. Often, when we spoke, we'd both be frustrated by how little I really knew about my childhood. I was desperate to know more and James said it would be helpful for him to know what I had gone through.

'You can ask for your files,' he said.

'What?'

'Your social-work files. You're entitled to see them. You can apply for them via a Freedom of Information request.'

I hadn't realized this before.

The same week I cut off contact with my family I got in touch with Birmingham City Council about accessing my files. A woman I spoke to on the phone sent out the forms to fill in. I entered my name, date of birth, addresses, my mother's details – anything that would help them get hold of the relevant documents.

I handed the form in at the neighbourhood office, where there was also a social-services office. It would be six to eight weeks before I could see the files.

It was only then that the enormity of what I had done regarding my family hit me. I suffered a massive breakdown. As before Christmas, when I'd been having dark days, I shut myself in the wardrobe, but this time it was far worse. When I emerged, I lay on the settee, incapable of moving. I wasn't sleeping, I wasn't eating. I couldn't seem to move. It was as if my body was shutting down, as if I was grieving for the family I never had. I missed my mother, craved her love. It was a process I had to go through.

This lasted into February. I wasn't any use to anyone. It was like I was in a regression. I'd gone back to being a child. I don't remember much about it, but everything was going on at once.

Finally, I was diagnosed as bipolar – capable of experiencing euphoric highs but also earth-shattering lows. I was put on new medication, and that helped a bit. It meant I could sleep, it relaxed me a little. I resumed my sessions with James and started having home treatments. James said this was a defining moment for me. Although it was hard – both for me and my family – I would be able to look back and see what a significant point this had been in my life, he said.

Slowly, I started dragging myself out of the black hole I was in. I got stronger and stronger and at the back of my head a voice said, 'They are not going to beat me.'

At the end of February I got a call from a lady at social services. She had my files. Did I want to go and collect them?

This was it. I braced myself for what I was going to discover.

Scott and I went up to the council offices and were shown into a little side room. There were two ladies there, and they handed me a brown envelope.

'What's that?' I asked.

'That's your files,' one of them said. 'Do you want to take them out and read them here?'

'No, I'll take them with me,' I said.

Scott and I looked at each other. Something wasn't right.

We got home and took out the pages. At first I thought there was more than there turned out to be, because there were three copies of each page, but then I realized there were only sixteen pages – only one for every year of my life as a child.

Reading through the pages, I discovered some horrifying realities. Rather than being taken into care when I was about eighteen months old, I had first come to the attention of social services when I was less than three months old.

The document said my mother was someone of 'quite low intelligence' and 'unreliable'. My father was said to be a named 'Anglo-Asian' man. The files also referred to Mother's relationship with Phil and confirmed what I thought – that he had been willing to accept me as his own child, despite my mother's dalliances with other men.

I was placed on a three-year supervision order at the age of eighteen months after being removed from

Mother's care on a Place of Safety Order after we had been found homeless by police late at night in the flat of a man who was subsequently arrested.

The papers detailed how Mother switched between three men and once fled to Scotland with one of them. By the time I was two Mother had spent time with two other men, one of whom was in prison, before moving on to another recently released from jail.

The incident when I fell out of the window aged three and suffered an injured leg and a fractured skull was referred to briefly. Although a care conference was held about that incident it appears I was returned to Mother's care without so much as a warning. At the time I was described as being an 'attractive and usually cheerful and amenable child who does not, as yet, present any problems or seem to be affected by her mother's lifestyle'.

As I read on I saw reports that neighbours had claimed I was being left alone in the flat while Mother was 'out soliciting'. The files went on to say that there was 'insufficient proof' regarding Mother's prostitution.

So there it was. Not that I needed confirmation. I knew well enough. But here in black and white was confirmation of my own sketchy memories and what relatives had told me. So that was what was happening when I went with Mother to visit those men. The documents might say there was insufficient evidence, but I knew the truth. My mother was a prostitute.

As I read on, more alarming testimony relating to my

childhood was revealed. Mother was arrested twice, on charges of criminal damage. There was an allegation that she had a conviction for prostitution.

As for the time I could remember being placed into foster care, the files contained reports that stated that I had mentioned Mother's behaviour – 'Mummy being naughty' – had spoken about 'having a new daddy' and said that Mother 'broke bottles and chased people with them'. I remained in care while various checks were made. Confirmation came that Mother had been cautioned for prostitution, but she had no convictions. At the end of the process it seemed that social services felt it was acceptable for me to be returned to Mother's care. She was given a list of orders to comply with and, even though she continually breached them, I remained in her care.

When I finished reading the files – which jumped from 1982 to 1985 and then to 1992, I realized there was a lot missing.

'This isn't right,' I said to Scott. 'There are events that I remember that aren't in here.'

I rang social services and asked about the missing files.

I was told that I couldn't see all of my files because, if matters related to a third party, I wasn't allowed to.

'But this is about me,' I said. 'I should be able to read my files.'

'I'm sorry,' the woman said. 'We can't help you.'

I spoke to Scott's sister, Rachel, who urged me to keep pursuing it.

'It's your right, Col,' she said, 'to know what happened to you.'

She recommended we ask the Citizens Advice Bureau. They gave me the names of solicitors and said I could try going down the legal route.

One of the firms on the list was Irwin Mitchell. I rang up and spoke to a solicitor called Luke Daniels. He agreed to meet me.

I took the files in and he looked at them.

'Where are the rest of them?' he asked.

'This is it.'

He asked me what episodes I could remember that weren't referred to in the documents. I told him about the time the school called in social services about my bruises and various other incidents I could recall.

'I think you have a case,' he said, and contacted the council and requested the rest of my files.

In May 2011 a woman from my lawyer's office rang to say they had received them and that I could come and collect them.

Finally.

When I got the call, I went cold. I was now going to find out the truth.

I took the train to Luke's office to pick them up. For some reason, Scott wasn't with me, which in itself was strange because he wouldn't have liked the thought of me collecting them on my own.

Waiting for me were two huge white lever-arch binders packed with documents. I couldn't believe it. I had been expecting a few files, but not this. I had to pop into a shop to get a carrier bag; otherwise it would have been difficult for me to get them home.

As I sat on the train part of me was desperate to read them but the other half wanted to put them under the seat and forget about them.

I twisted the plastic-bag handles round my fingers, turning them purple. The pain took my mind off what I was about to read.

Only when I got off the train and started the five-minute walk back to my house did I start to panic. What was I going to read? I knew there were bits missing from the original set of files, but these folders were huge. Obviously, a lot more had gone on in my childhood than I'd thought.

I got inside the house, tucked the bag behind the sofa and tried to forget about the files until Scott came home. When he arrived back the first thing he did was hug me. I so needed that. I collapsed into his arms, saying nothing.

We got on with what needed to be done: I cooked tea, the girls showered and were settled for the night, and I made the sandwiches for their lunch the next day.

Scott disappeared upstairs and, after ten minutes, he called me up. He had lit candles, made me a hot drink and gently plumped my pillows. I sat on the bed and prepared myself.

Inside these files was the truth about my childhood.

Oh my God.

What the hell would they reveal?

23

I had to read them on my own. It was something I needed to do. Scott was always there in the house – James had advised me to have him there – but he left me to digest the information on my own. Every now and then he would pop up to the bedroom with another coffee and a hug.

The first binder contained pages 1 to 294. The other had pages 295 to 633.

On the very first page, although there was no date and much of it was blacked out to protect 'third parties', it said that I was 'being cared for by a succession of friends and relatives' in 'various houses'.

My mother came back drunk and with a boyfriend one Saturday morning to collect me from a flat. At the foot of the page I could make out, in spidery writing: 'Police were concerned about care of child.'

The next entry stated that I was admitted to a care facility on 29 January 1979 when I was sixteen months old. It said the chain of events that led me there seemed to 'lack clarity'. Detail about my mother was blacked out but it seemed that action had been taken because the police were concerned about how I was being cared for.

In an assessment of my condition, the report said

I was under-stimulated, had not been potty-trained and 'was more at home eating with [my] fingers'.

On 19 February that year an interim care order had been granted for me. Amid more blackings-out it gave hints that Mother was living with someone and that she was refusing access to someone who was my 'putative father'.

The following month I was placed on a three-year supervision order.

From 1979 to July 1983 I was in care, with a succession of home leaves and a home trial where Mother was given the chance to prove her worthiness as a parent.

As I read on, it became clear that the social services had been concerned about my wellbeing as early as three months after I was born, when it appeared that Mother wasn't feeding me properly. A social worker had been refused entry to the house. By the time I was five and a half months old I had been in hospital twice and seemed to respond better to feeding in there than at home.

As I'd read in the first lot of files, all these events happened far earlier than anyone had ever told me.

Reading the files was a frustrating process. Many of the pages were incorrectly filed and the dates of entries sometimes fluctuated wildly. Every time Scott came into the room to see how I was doing I would offload a whole heap of misdemeanours and failures: it would almost have been hysterical if it wasn't so sad. Certain words would jump off the page, and I found myself reading sentences over and over again. In some parts I questioned what I was reading. Half of it I didn't remember, and in those instances it was like I was reading about another child. It was quite disturbing. I always thought my memory had got the better of me: it always reminded me of stuff from my past that I'd rather forget – I hated it – but, as I read my files I began to think that maybe my mind had blocked the worst from my memory banks.

I found it extremely harrowing. I could only manage a few pages at a time before I had to stop and try to digest what I'd just read.

Some entries went over my earliest days in more detail.

Information was being drip-fed to me. In a report written by a key social worker, Penny, the one I remembered getting to know and who I named my puppy after, she stated that I had come to the attention of the department in 1977 because of my 'apparent failure to thrive'.

As I had read in the first lot of files, 'Mother was reported as being of quite low intelligence and unreliable,' she wrote. My birth weight was 5lb 9oz. At three weeks old, I was found to be cold, I had thrush in my mouth and very severe thrush on my buttocks. By February 1978, when I was just five months old, someone – presumably Mother, but again much of the text was redacted – was feeding me on pasteurized milk and potatoes and gravy. In March of that year social services were aware that I was living in a flat without a fireguard. Mother received £6 to buy one but spent the money on 'other household items'. There was a request for a further £8.65 for another. In August there was an entry that said there were concerns about where I was living. The details were blacked out, however. Whoever it was I was living with, they were entertaining visitors until the early hours of the morning, and neighbours had complained about the noise. Social services said then that there was nothing they could do as there was 'no concern at present re childcare'.

An alarming set of circumstances emerged in the entries from January 1979. I had been staying with different people, none of whom had had a legal right to care for me. Mother appeared to had snatched me from the house of a boyfriend's parents. Police spent a weekend trying to arrest Mother's then boyfriend. When they found me, I had no cot and no blankets.

In an eleven-page report, the original social worker, who featured a lot in the files, listed the times she had chased up my wellbeing and confronted Mother, from April to May 1979. A further six-page report from May to September that same year showed how the same social worker tried to get Mother to see me on my birthday. She brought me a nightdress and slippers but social workers observed she had 'little real patience' with me. On another occasion Mother said she would visit to please the social worker.

In June 1979 it was reported that I was the subject of a 28-day Place of Safety Order. At the time I was meant to be in a children's home in Castle Vale, but had been missing since earlier that month. We had been in Scotland with a mystery man. In November, Penny recommended short-term foster care. Apparently, I cried as much when she left me as when Mother did.

In February 1980 Mother was given a rehabilitation plan, where she had to prove her reliability in order to continue being allowed to see me. In week one she was granted five visits, this was repeated for four weeks. In week six, if the previous weeks had gone well, she would be allowed to have me overnight.

The results showed that she visited me just two days that first week; in week two, three days; in week three she only managed two days again; while in week four she saw me for just one day.

Further on, I learned that the case conference report stated that, although Mother attended only four out of ten meetings and had no concept that I had been kept waiting and was left disappointed, they still agreed to let her take me home.

When Mother told me I was going home, social services acknowledged that I had wet the bed several times. I also said to another foster child that I didn't want to go home. They said they reluctantly allowed me to go 'home on trial' and that Mother had done just enough to fulfil the contract, there being insufficient evidence to keep me in care with a view to adoption.

I couldn't believe it. There it was in black and white. Social services had given Mother strict conditions, which she blatantly flouted, yet still she got her own way.

As I read on I saw that in January 1979 a foster mother had looked at taking me long term but had then found me too much to cope with in addition to her own three children.

As I had read in the initial sixteen pages I had received, I was made the subject of the three-year supervision order in March 1979 after police found Mother and me homeless late at night. Although her name was blotted out it was clear I would only be put back into Mother's care 'when she had demonstrated considerably more stability in her lifestyle than in recent months'.

In a summary of my case it stated that from the period of March 1979 to June that year Mother moved home at least seven times, involving 'four different men friends'.

On 21 January 1980 a grant was made to buy Mother a travel card so she could visit me.

This report contained details of the fall I had from Mother's flat window. It said, 'Collette suffered an accident in September 1980 when she fell from the window of the flat, suffering a leg injury and fractured skull.' It went on to state that I had shown no distress at separation from my mother; the only noticeable reaction had been one wet bed.

Nearly two hundred pages into the files came further

details of my fall. In September 1980 West Midlands Police reported that I fell from the first-floor window at about 10 a.m. It said, 'She was able to reach the window and open it by standing on mother's bed while mother was asleep and fell through. Flat is very small and is not fully suitable for young child: it is desirable that safety catch should be fitted to this window if Collette is to return there when she is eventually discharged from hospital.'

Later on in the files I read the social worker's report into the incident. According to the sergeant who attended the scene, Mother had been out at a party, leaving a boyfriend babysitting. She returned at 3 a.m. and went to bed. In the morning the boyfriend left, leaving her in bed. It went on, 'Collette got into her bed. The next thing she knew a neighbour brought Collette up in her arms, [Collette] having fallen out of the window.'

When the social worker spoke to Mother the story had changed. Mother said she'd got up to make a cup of tea and called me repeatedly but was unable to discover where I was hiding. Then a neighbour brought me up. Mother said I seemed quite cheerful and in fact laughed. Then I started crying and she called an ambulance. The social worker asked about the boyfriend but Mother said he wasn't living there and was just a friend.

In September 1980 an entry stated that someone (the name was redacted) felt that 'Collette should be taken away from her mother.' He said that 'on occasions

Collette is left in the flat all night on her own'. I was only three years old.

Some of the most traumatic episodes for me to digest concerned this period. Far on in the files were reports that stated I had once been left with a 'babysitter who suffered three fits in quarter of an hour'. I was taken to the police station while officers traced my mother.

Around the same time, it was written, 'Collette is often in the street "running after men".' Someone, perhaps a neighbour, was concerned that I could 'get picked up'. There were further concerns, at that time, from a neighbour, who said, 'Collette is often out in the street with "nothing on". She follows people up and down the street and talks to anyone.' Someone – again a neighbour, most likely – had also seen me 'soiling on the landing of the flats and wiping it up with her pants'.

When I read that, I was heartbroken. I thought of my precious daughters and how I would feel if they were left to fend for themselves in that sort of squalor, forced to clean up after themselves and not potty-trained. Why did no one help me?

Social workers were then informed that I was telling people, 'Mummy's going to hide me.' The suggestion was that Mother might have been planning to take me to Liverpool. It also said I was 'left with various men'.

On another occasion, still around the same time, a witness said they saw me again 'standing on the window-sill of the flat'. It was a miracle I didn't have another accident.

Still around this time, Mother was once again warned she was in danger of losing me, but she continued to go out every night. Another witness said Mother 'slap[ped me] harshly without real cause'.

In August 1981, when I was still three, a case conference heard that a neighbour had alleged that I was left alone at night. Social workers were not able to substantiate these claims but the report added that 'there is no doubt that the child has been left with a number of different inadequate babysitters'.

It was alleged that Mother 'stayed in bed and left Collette to wander the streets'. Mother denied this to police, who said they had no evidence to suggest the flat was being used for prostitution. Once again, Mother's word was taken as gospel.

Further entries from 1981 stated that I was often let out into the street on my own.

'Collette had made various comments about her mother's behaviour, i.e. "mummy being naughty", having a new Daddy and that her mother "broke bottles and chased people with them".' This was in March 1982. I was four.

Around the same time, a social worker reported that I had told her, 'Mummy used to get me out of bed, sit me on her lap and then hit me a lot and make my nose bleed.' There was no word on how this serious allegation of abuse was followed up.

Notes from a case conference into my situation dated 5 April 1982 referred to me being in a foster home. They stated that, when Mother phoned me, her calls were very self-centred. She asked if I missed her and told me she had a 'present for her in the form of a new Pakistani daddy'. It was noted that I showed no signs of anxiety on being separated from my mother.

The headmistress of my infant school told those assembled at the case conference that she had received an unsubstantiated report from another family to the effect that someone – I assume my mother – had got me out of bed and hit me, making my nose bleed. Apparently, I corroborated the story, but there had been no previous evidence of child abuse. The notes stated that those at the meeting could not agree on the best course of action, so a decision was deferred until they could consult with police.

At a meeting with social services in 1982 I fell and bumped my head and was crying. Although some details were blacked out, it seemed clear that Mother made no effort to comfort me and, in fact, I turned to Penny, the social worker, for 'physical comfort'.

I also read about the time in July 1982 when Penny took me to my mother's registry-office wedding.

Apparently, I said 'fifteen times' that I didn't want to go home to Mother; it was also stated that I had wet the bed frequently in the weeks leading up to the point when I did go back to her.

There was a reference to a female police officer expressing concern in 1983 of 'Collette being in moral danger', because of someone living there. The name was again redacted, but why did no one follow it up?

And then, finally, came the nub of the matter. After the case conference in 1983 the reason it was decided that I should remain in Mother's care despite 'serious concern' about her 'ability to provide the stability and security' I needed was because the 'City Solicitors Office indicated Department's case weak' should my mother attempt an appeal.

And so rehabilitation was 'reluctantly agreed'. There it was. Faceless suits who had never met me sat in judgement of my case, despite social workers raising their concerns repeatedly.

That was where the failure in my case lay.

And there was more and more. In 1983 there was mention that Mother had asked me whether she should keep her unborn baby. I was five at the time. It was added that Mother 'didn't seem to see anything wrong in putting this problem to Collette'.

On one occasion in 1984 I had a leg injury caused by a hot iron. No one spoke to me about it. A man then came to my school to have his picture taken with me but no attempts were made to establish his identity.

Foster carers were lined up to take me in 1984 should my mother and stepfather be imprisoned. The files did not reveal what the pair might have gone to jail for but, because they weren't put in prison, nothing was done.

On another occasion I was burned in a bath of hot

water. Even though I told my foster carers at the time I did not want to stay with my mother, I was again returned to her care.

One entry dated June 1987 told of an incident when social services were called to my school after I had suffered one particularly bad beating. Despite there being a suggestion that 'Child abuse procedures [were] implemented', nothing seemed to be followed up.

Reading further still, I came across another reference to the school visit by social services. It turned out the teacher did not think I merited a medical and she was unconcerned because she had a more 'serious emergency on her hands'.

The papers said that, following the school's examination, there was 'concern over the relationship between Collette and her mother and that Collette was frightened and upset which we felt was because of her mother'. It continued, 'The main concern was emotional neglect. The team manager's decision was to have a case conference.'

Other documents charted how social services tried to come to the house three times, but there was no reply. When they finally did manage to conduct a home visit they reported that the family were 'not willing to accept social work involvement and they will be changing Collette's school'.

Of course, I knew how that happened – but why didn't anyone speak to me in private? There just seemed to be an acceptance of my parents' version of events.

The files then jumped to 1992, with a report, from the time when I was fourteen, saying that 'Collette came to see her saying she has had enough of her mother who hits and bites her and treats her differently to other children. It is worse when her stepdad isn't around as he protects her from her mother.'

It was interesting to read that my stepdad was supposedly protecting me from my mother. Certainly she could be brutal when he wasn't around.

Some of the entries surprised me. In an entry dated February 1993 it was revealed that social services knew about the incident when I was raped. In the files it was described as an 'attempted indecent assault' by '10 youths'. When I'd spoken to the police I hadn't given a full statement about what had happened, but I had no idea that the police had passed the information on to the social services. I was stunned that there had been no follow-up inquiry to see if I was OK.

Elsewhere in the files was a reference to Mother and my stepdad approaching the housing department with a complaint concerning racial harassment. This seemed to relate to their request for a new house.

I had to read nearly to the end of the second volume of files to find any reference to me being beaten by my stepdad. Amid a raft of blacked-out lines, he was actually named. It came in a report following a home visit by social workers in April 1986. The report stated that Mother was saying that she was going to get rid of Dave. It added, 'Told him he was not going to hit Collette.' It went on, 'Collette said she was afraid of XXXX. He was always hitting her. Collette started to cry.'

If social services were in possession of that report in 1986, why did they do nothing when my parents removed me from school amid the claims of beatings just a year later?

When I had finished reading through both files I had to try to absorb all the events that had made me the person I had become. So harrowing was the experience – and so painful the revelations – that it took me two weeks to get through them all.

Once I'd absorbed the information, the overriding feeling I had was anger. At first it was aimed solely at the social-work department. From birth until I was sixteen they had been aware of so much – neglect, abuse, sexual abuse – yet they did nothing. All the time, they knew what was going on. I had a teacher at secondary school who was in constant contact with social services. I didn't know this until I read my files. When I was fifteen I had begged them to please take me away from my mother. She had bitten me, scratched me, pulled out clumps of my hair. The social worker told me to go back to school and speak to the teacher.

It was page after page of failings.

Some teachers were also complicit. Even the police. They were aware of Mother's lifestyle. They had numerous meetings with social workers and teachers and heard allegations on so many occasions but, aside from passing on the complaints, they did little to help me.

I was also angry at how much my family knew. Suddenly, I had evidence that challenged their accounts of their role in my upbringing. So many people were to blame – not just my mum.

There were times when I had sat and listened to relatives telling me all the bad things my mother did, but when I read the files it mentioned times when I was left at a police station by those same relatives, who had claimed they had been looking after me.

I wanted to say to them, 'Why couldn't you help? Why did you leave me at a police station? Why couldn't you look after me?'

So many people were to blame.

Now it was time to get justice.

24

There she was . . . in front of me. There was nowhere for her to run. Forced to answer question after question about how she mistreated me, how she abandoned me, how she left me with strange men, left me to fend for myself, left me sitting in my own mess, had me wandering the streets on my own as a toddler. It was to go on for four hours. Every painstaking detail pored over, every event relived – but this time with her in the dock. Why did she hit me for no reason? How did it feel for me to have more affection for a social worker than for my own flesh and blood? What gave her the right to expose me to sex-for-cash sessions, to violent partners?

Finally, I would get answers.

These exchanges took place only in my head, but they felt so real. I could almost taste my satisfaction in watching her squirm.

After Luke, the lawyer, saw the files, he knew straight away I had a case. However, he spoke to a barrister in London for a second opinion. He believed we also had a strong case so, within months of receiving the files, my lawyer informed Birmingham City Council we would be lodging a complaint against them.

I was initially sceptical about taking a case against the council. Birmingham City Council is the largest local authority in Europe, and we were talking about decisions that were made over thirty years earlier.

Taking legal action wasn't my motivation for wanting to access my files. I just wanted answers. I wanted Mother to explain herself. I wanted the council held accountable. However, part of me also worried that I was making too much of it. I had survived this long, hadn't I? But if the lawyers believed I had been failed and wanted to take the case, who was I to argue? Plus, it had ceased to be just about me. How many other children out there had been failed by social services? My case was believed to be the first of its kind in the UK. If I was successful, it might stop similar failures happening again.

Another important consequence of getting my files was that I decided to try to take action against my sexual abusers, who for years had evaded justice. Simon, the married man, had since died of a heart attack, I heard, but Adam was still alive. I went to the police and told them what had happened when he babysat for me.

Although my allegations were historical, the police arrested Adam. He admitted being my babysitter but denied any impropriety. The police also took a statement from Donna. She knew what had gone on and told the police, but as she was not a witness to the abuse she could not corroborate my claims.

The police then went to my mother. If she confirmed she had left me alone with him, then it would corroborate his own assertion that he was my babysitter, and the fact that he was left alone with me would give greater weight to my allegations in court.

Mother denied ever leaving me in his care. I hadn't spoken to her since I had cut off contact back in January. This wasn't about standing up for me, this was about telling the truth. It was beyond her.

The police told me that without my mother's corroboration they had a slim chance of a conviction in court. My allegations would have to lie dormant.

I don't know why Mother chose to say what she did, but I suspect she was trying to protect herself. At the time, her health was deteriorating rapidly. Although the operation had been a success, her cancer had returned, and more aggressively this time. I was still receiving updates on her condition from family friends, but the same relatives who just months earlier had been only too happy to tell me what a bad mother she was were now flocking to her bedside.

I didn't know what to make of the information I got from friends of the family that Mother was fading. I could scarcely believe it. After all, I'd seen her beat a brain tumour once before. The woman was indestructible, was she not?

In July 2012 my lawyers made significant progress with the case. They had handed my files to an independent social-work expert to give a report on whether, in her professional opinion, Birmingham City Council had breached the duty of care owed to me when I was a child.

Her findings were startling. She believed the council failed when Mother did not comply with the rehabilitation programme. According to her, I should have been placed in foster care for longer.

In 1983, when teachers reported that I had been slapped, and then when I changed schools and it was noted I had turned up with a black eye, the expert said the council fell below standards of practice laid down for the social services.

After listing twenty entries of concern in my notes, she concluded that I should not have been returned to my mother's care in 1982 and said that if I had been permanently removed from her I would have fulfilled my potential and could have been protected from harm. She ended her report by saying that 'the service provided to you by Birmingham City Council fell below the standards expected of them at the time you were under their care'.

It was a crucial development. It meant I wasn't imagining it. I had been failed by social services.

On the back of her report a consultation was arranged with a barrister in London for that September.

Before then, in early August, I discovered I was expecting again. Scott and I were thrilled and we hoped a new baby would complete our family.

I was six weeks into the pregnancy, however, when I received a phone call, at eight o'clock on a Thursday night. It was the daughter of a family friend who had been at the hospital visiting my mother.

'Collette,' she said, 'I'm sorry. Your mum died half an hour ago.'

25

No. It can't be. She can't be gone. Not now. Not when I was so close to putting her on the stand.

I stood there cold and numb. I wanted to feel some sort of emotion but none came. She had won.

All this time I had wanted answers. All this time I had thought nothing could kill her, and now she was gone.

I imagined her somewhere laughing at me. Her final humiliation. I felt utterly flattened.

When I told my children their nan had died there was no emotion from them. They didn't care. Tamzin, whose life Mother had tried to make miserable, just said, 'Oh, well.'

Seeing their reaction stirred something inside me. I tried to instil in them some feeling, as much for my own benefit. 'She's your biological nan and you don't care that she's no longer around?'

The following day, Rachel, Scott's sister, was going into hospital for a biopsy. Normally, she would have been the first person in whom I would have confided but that day wasn't the day to tell her about my mother.

Devastatingly, it was confirmed Rachel had melanoma, a deadly skin cancer. Guiltily, I was more upset about her predicament than my mother's passing.

A post-mortem was being carried out, so Mother's body was lying in the chapel of rest in the hospital. The family had all been going there to pay their last respects. I knew I wasn't welcome but on Monday morning I rang the hospital.

I explained to a nurse that I hadn't seen my mother for over a year and I knew that she was ill but I'd been told to keep away. 'She died, and I'll understand if you say no but is there any chance I could come and say goodbye to her?' I asked.

'Of course you can,' she said. 'She's your mum. Just let me make sure the family's not going to be here.'

The nurse was brilliant. She called back and said, 'The family are coming up this morning but I've made sure no one comes up this afternoon. I've told them we are too busy. So if you come up this afternoon, come up any time and your mum will be ready for you.'

Scott and Sally accompanied me to the hospital. Sally waited outside. Scott came with me into the chapel of rest but let me speak to her alone.

When the nurse pulled the sheet off her body Mother was holding a little teddy bear. 'She said it was yours,' the nurse said.

I knew that the nurse only put the bear there for me, but in my mind I saw it as a final message from my mother – that she was saying she did love me after all.

Standing there in the chapel of rest, the feelings I experienced were so scrambled. I felt sick. Mother looked so peaceful and silent, but I couldn't prevent my anger building.

I had lost my mother, but this woman had got away with what she had done to me. I would never get my day with her, never get my chance to see if she was sorry.

I stared at her lying on the cold steel bed and my heart sank further. A sudden feeling of guilt washed over me. She had died thinking I hated her when, really, that couldn't be any further from the truth.

'I had to find out the truth,' I said aloud, although there was no one beside me to hear. 'Why didn't you love me?'

Then the words started to flow. They got louder and louder. It was as if I was that child again but for the first time I was standing up to her.

'I know I should, but I don't hate you,' I said, to her cold, lifeless body. 'You're my mum and no one will ever replace you in my heart. And, in a strange way, I forgive you. I blame the others for letting us both down. Now, rest in peace, Mum. I'll see you soon. Love you.'

I turned round and left.

Her funeral was held at the crematorium that week. My girls wanted to go to it, but again, I knew I would not be welcome. I also knew many of my relatives would be expecting me to show up to cause a scene. As much as it pained me not to be at my own mother's funeral, I wasn't going to give them the satisfaction.

Instead, my family invited Graham, even though he hadn't seen his own children for years by that point.

In a way I had made my peace with Mother, but I was still angry with the family members who had betrayed me.

Once the funeral was over, however, I had to focus on my own situation. I had a baby growing inside me who I had to stay strong for, and a husband and sister-in-law who needed me.

To support my case, an independent psychiatrist assessed me. When he'd read through my file and analysed me, he said, 'I don't understand how you are still here today.'

His report was added to the claim against the council. He confirmed that my bipolar and associated conditions followed a 'catastrophic experience' and stated that I suffered physical injuries and their consequences at the time of the abuse. He stated that I had suffered flashbacks, nightmares and periods of disassociation since beginning to come to terms with the childhood abuse.

The report said, 'The claimant has taken overdoses. She had relationships with two violent and controlling men. Her attraction to them and her self-harming behaviour are attributable to her abusive childhood.'

In January 2013 Birmingham City Council responded, denying that the social workers had been negligent. It argued that the action they had taken could be considered reasonable.

My lawyers proceeded with the claim. The council

wanted me to see an independent psychiatrist of their choosing. I was heavily pregnant at the time. Their stance was clear. While they couldn't deny neglect, they tried to say that my current mental problems had nothing to do with the mental torture I had suffered in my childhood. My depression and multiple overdoses had nothing to do with my past.

Meanwhile, Rachel's health deteriorated rapidly. On 4 March 2013 we went to say our goodbyes to her because we were told she wasn't going to make it through the night.

Mercifully, she held on, and on the following day I gave birth to my fourth daughter. It was a happy time because she was what everybody needed, but at the same time it was very sad because of Rachel. In fact, we called our precious new baby Codey-Rachel.

I had to stay in hospital for two days until doctors were satisfied that the medication I was on hadn't gone into the baby's system. It was hard, because my mum, despite what had happened between us, had always been one of the first ones there after the births of my other three girls. She had held them and given me presents for them. Lying in hospital with my newborn girl, I missed her terribly.

When I was discharged I immediately went to Rachel and spent the rest of that afternoon with my dear sister-in-law. She was delighted we were carrying on her name with our daughter. 'You've made my day,' she said.

A week after Codey was born I got a phone call. It was Luke.

'I have some good news,' he said. 'Birmingham City Council have offered to settle out of court.'

I could scarcely believe what I was hearing. In the last correspondence we had received from their lawyers they had seemed determined to fight it out in court.

'What does this mean?' I said.

'Well, let me find out what financial settlement they are offering and I'll come back to you.'

He rang back.

'They're offering £20,000 compensation,' Luke said. 'They're not apologizing or admitting wrongdoing, but they have been advised by their lawyers to settle. What do you think?'

I couldn't believe it. A council the size of Birmingham offering to settle with me?

'What are my options?' I asked.

'We can reject this offer,' Luke said. 'I'm still confident we will win in court and the damages could be higher. However, in court you will have to give evidence and I'm worried how you'll be, having to withstand hours of questioning, particularly being cross-examined by their QC. It could be rough on you.'

It was something I'd thought about. When she was alive, I had imagined what it would be like to see Mother squirm on the stand, but I had also contemplated how I would feel, having to relive every incident, my memory tested, my version of events picked over by a highly skilled barrister. It could be terrifying, possibly worse than having to live through it at the time.

This offer was hard to take in. On one hand, I was relieved there was an end in sight – one that didn't require me to give evidence in court. On the other, I was disappointed that the council was not accepting that it had failed me and was not apologizing.

It was also hard to get excited. The money didn't interest me. That wasn't why I was doing this. I was doing it, hopefully, to set a precedent – to make social services change their practices. Plus, I was so preoccupied with my new baby and we had been beside ourselves with grief about Rachel, I could barely focus on anything else.

'Yes,' I said. 'Let's take it.'

Rachel battled bravely on until 24 March but lost her fight. We were all devastated.

When I cut off contact with my parents Rachel was the one I confided in. She was a wonderful listener: she never told me the things I should or shouldn't do; she kept her opinions to herself. That's what I loved about her. 'You do what you need to do,' she would say, 'and I'll be here for you.'

She was also the one who had urged me to pursue the case. I didn't get the chance to tell her I'd won. In the end, she was too poorly to take in news like that, but I know she would have been thrilled for me.

I had not really grieved over my mother dying, so when Rachel passed on, I think my grief was a combination for the two of them. Rachel was cremated at the same place my mother was, and it felt like I was saying goodbye to two people that day.

Two weeks later the council settled, as its lawyers had promised. In a statement, the council said it was a 'difficult case' and that it was 'sympathetic' to my feelings.

It added, 'Social-work decisions are often very difficult when you're faced with judgements involving removing children from their parents. In this case, the council did not accept that its decisions were wrong. However, the case has been settled on the basis of legal advice.'

The independent psychiatrist for the council had agreed with our assessment. Once that happened, its lawyers felt they had no option but to settle out of court.

When I finally had a chance to take in what had happened, I was relieved. Finally, thirty-five years after that little baby girl came to the attention of the social-services department, someone had listened to what she had to say.

I had a voice after all.

Now, I was determined to use it.

Epilogue

'The immediate position is unsafe for children and needs immediate action.' Those were not the words from my legal complaint against Birmingham City Council, or of any independent expert. Those were the words of the council's Director of Children's Services. And they were not uttered in the 1970s, when the city's social-services department first failed me, but in 2013, after a series of systematic failures.

In a presentation to city councillors, he added, 'There needs to be greater confidence that concerns are heard and responded to – from staff and about children.'

Mr Hay was talking after the council's settlement in my case – believed to be the first of its kind in the UK. He wasn't talking specifically about me. Sadly, I am not an isolated case. Birmingham City Council has presided over several shockingly disturbing cases.

In 2008, a serious case review found that the death of Khyra Ishaq, a seven-year-old girl who died weighing less than three stone and suffering from pneumonia and meningitis, could have been prevented. The review highlighted a lack of communication between her school, social workers and other agencies. Social workers did not listen to concerns from school staff about Khyra, and concerns voiced by two members of the public were not acted upon.

In June 2013, just two months after the council settled my case, the shocking story of Keanu Williams emerged, also from Birmingham. The two-year-old boy was beaten to death by his mother, Rebecca Shuttleworth, who had subjected him to months of cruelty.

Shuttleworth apparently convinced her support worker that she had turned her life around. Instead, the abuse and neglect had lasted five months, including a terrifying last assault that caused Keanu's death. Birmingham Children's Services acknowledged that chances to save the boy had been missed.

Failures of social services are not restricted to Birmingham. From Coventry, in September 2013, came the tragic story of Daniel Pelka, a four-year-old boy who died from a head injury in March 2012 after months of starvation, poisoning and abuse. It was one of the worst cases of child abuse in Britain since the Baby P tragedy five years earlier. A review into his death found that Coventry Children's Services wrongly concluded on four separate occasions that Daniel was safe at home after conducting supposedly rigorous assessments, although workers never actually spoke to the boy.

Daniel's mother, Magdalena Luczak, and her boyfriend, Mariusz Krezolek, were jailed for life for torturing and murdering her son. However, the case review suggested that few lessons from the Baby P case had been learned. It described Daniel as 'invisible' to child-protection professionals who were distracted by his mother's problems with depression and alcohol abuse. It painted a picture of a chaotic and violent home and a mother who dragged her children through a string of drunken relationships with three men.

All these cases sounded shockingly familiar to me.

In each of them – and in the case of Baby P, who died after his abuse by his mother and her boyfriend went undetected by Haringey social services – there was a failure of the system. Social workers were not solely to blame, however. A breakdown in communication and a failure to act on the part of teachers, healthcare workers and sometimes even police led to these tragic deaths.

I was lucky. By rights, I should be dead – another tragic episode which would prompt a serious case review. I fell out of a first-floor window, was burned, battered and left with paedophiles. When I was assessed by the independent psychiatrist during the preparation of my case, he said, 'I don't understand how you are still here today.'

Sometimes, neither do I. I might have survived everything my mother could throw at me, but there were many times I tried to end it all. I took twelve overdoses in all and, at times, only the intervention of friends saved me.

Perhaps I survived for a reason – to highlight the failings of our care professionals and to speak for the victims who have been silenced for ever.

Since my case became public I have been inundated

with messages from people who have also been failed by the system. The number of people with stories to tell is unbelievable. I always say to them, 'Look, you have survived. That's the amazing thing.'

My fight for justice did not end with the settlement. Birmingham City Council has so far refused to apologize for the way I was let down. I want them to admit they got things wrong and I want them to be reviewing all their cases to make sure the same thing does not happen to others.

This is why I am working with Action For Children and Jack Dromey MP to have the law changed to recognize the impact child abuse has on a victim's mental health. Presently, the law only recognizes physical injuries, but the impact on a person's mental state can be far worse. Those scars can take much longer to heal and can stay with victims for the rest of their lives.

As part of my treatment, doctors diagnosed that I am suffering from post-traumatic stress disorder. That gives you a sense of the impact that years of abuse, in any form, has on a victim.

I have continued to remain out of contact with my family. It's a high price to pay for my own wellbeing, but if I had not taken that drastic action I know I would still be running around after them. I would still be that little girl seeking their approval.

In the end, my mother discovered that what goes around comes around. Karma bit her on the backside massively. She discovered what it is like when the tormentor becomes the tormented. It hit her hard. I don't think she ever thought about me and the impact her lifestyle had on me; she was too wrapped up in herself to notice.

It will always sadden me that she died thinking I hated her. That wasn't the case. She was always my mother. However, she had the chance to redeem herself when I reported my abuser to the police, and she chose not to take it. I can never forgive her for that.

I am determined to be the best mum I can be to my four wonderful daughters. I try to shower them with the love I never tasted. That will hopefully be one legacy of all of this suffering.

However, I will always have a huge mum-shaped hole in my own life. I've tried to fill it with other relatives and friends. My aunt Wendy, who took me in when I was fourteen after my mother tried to attack me with a knife, often filled that role but, sadly, she too died. Her friend Lorraine, a foster carer, is another who I look to for motherly advice. They have been wonderful to me.

Yet, while I am much better now, a part of me will always yearn for the thing I never had – my mother's love.

Acknowledgements

I wish to thank:

My girls, for teaching me the meaning of motherly love and for being the best. They are never naughty, so I never have to show my mother's gene. They allow me to fuss without complaining. Their love, understanding and the bond between us will keep me smiling until the day I die.

Scott, simply for loving me. All I ever wanted was someone to love me for me – no lies, no secrets, no hidden skeletons. The day I opened up to my husband was the day I became free. He taught me to love and trust. He is my best friend. He took all the verbal and physical abuse I lashed on to him and received the anger that had been building up. I have pushed him to the edge but he has stayed with me. Our marriage is based on more than the usual stuff. I opened my heart and soul to this man. He will always be a part of me.

Scott's family, for accepting my girls and me and for showing us that family love and loyalty really does exist. Family get-togethers are the best. I'm not just Scott's wife, I am a person with feelings and, whenever I need that hug or kick up the backside, I can turn to any one of them and they shower me with their love and understanding.

Jane, my angel, my closest friend, my confidante and my outer voice. She has picked me up so many times that I am no longer afraid to fall. She saved my life, she is my life, and that will never change.

Sharon, for dragging me out, giving me a social life and for always having the kettle on. She too has been through some nightmares. We bounce off one another and put the world to rights. I feel so protective towards her because she gets me. Jane and Sharon are the only outsiders I trust, not just with myself but with my girls. I love them always.

I also need to thank Rachel. She is no longer with us but it was her wise words and wisdom that gave me the strength to do what I have done. I still look to her for guidance and the void she left will always be great. She was a fantastic role model for my children and me and, although her beautiful boys will always carry on her memory, I will never forget the many things she did. She brought Scott and me together, and she gave the girls and me the family we never had.

Finally, I would like to thank Talk to the Press, Douglas Wight, Fenella Bates and all at Penguin for believing in me. Without their help I wouldn't have been able to tell my story.